DASH DIET
COOKBOOK
for beginners

QUICK AND EASY RECIPES FOR 365 DAYS TO START
A HEALTHY LIFE AND LOWER BLOOD PRESSURE

Maria Lacuoca

Table of Contents

Introduction

Generally speaking, most people who are looking to start the DASH diet are people who suffer from high blood pressure themselves or have a family member that does.

Men are going to be more likely to have hypertension issues, especially after the age of 45, and a significant amount of patients with diabetes will experience these symptoms as well. Also, put at risk are individuals who are overweight. However, hypertension can happen to anyone.

DASH is an acronym for Dietary Approaches to Stop Hypertension. The diet is centered on eating a balanced combination of lean meats, vegetables, whole grains, and fruits, and keeping sodium intake between two-thirds and one Tbsp of salt per day, depending on the reasons for starting the diet and the results you are seeking.

The DASH diet also focuses on keeping fats, added sugars, and red meat to a lower level. As with all diets, there is a happy medium for keeping true to the diet.

When you experience the symptoms of hypertension for extended amounts of time, you are more at risk for heart disease, kidney issues, and higher glucose levels leading to diabetes. You also are at a higher risk of early mortality.

However, following the simple-to-understand guidelines of the DASH Diet will help bring your blood pressure numbers to a more manageable level and help you be healthier in the long run, bringing your chances of living a much more fulfilling life for you.

When you work towards your goals on the DASH Diet, you will start to see the results rather quickly, which will help you to keep your willpower working towards your personal goals.

Chapter 1.

Definition and Some General Information

Dietary Approach to Stop Hypertension or DASH strategies is a diet for people who want to avoid or treat high blood pressure and reduce their risk of cardiovascular disease.

The DASH diet concentrates on fruit, whole grains, vegetables, and meats. The diet was created after researchers found that high blood pressure was much less common in people who consume an herbal diet, including vegans and vegetarians.

The DASH diet emphasizes vegetables and fruits with some lean protein sources such as fish, chicken, and beans. Scientists believe that one of the most significant explanations for this diet is that it reduces salt consumption.

This diet, also known as the 'healthy diet,' is intended to offer a real solution to high blood pressure by recommending a diet that simply controls the consumption of nutrients and does not change the common diet we're used to.

Dietary methods to avoid hypertension or Dash control the sodium and fat intake to maintain an individual's natural blood pressure. Dash aims to prepare a diet that serves nutritious meals, thus stopping people from eating between meals and causing food intake loss of control. As it prevents people from starving between meals, it hopefully becomes more satisfying and less controlled.

The Dash diet teaches people to complete a specific diet program by loading the kitchen with recommended food, preparing certain meals, and completing some workouts. Meal plans suggested by Dash typically contain high fiber, calcium, magnesium, and potassium ingredients. Dash diets go low on sugar and sodium, and stress the need to consume green leafy fruits and vegetables.

Avocado dip is one of today's most popular Dash diets due to its very convenient and inexpensive preparation. Among the many fruits highly recommended for the Dash diet, avocados are a very rich source of monosaturated fat and lutein (antioxidants that help protect vision). Avocado should be mashed and used in this recipe, mixed with fat-free sour cream, onion, and hot sauce. This dip is eaten with tortilla chips or vegetable slices.

A total of 65 calories, 2 grams protein, 5 grams of fat, 4 grams of carbohydrate, 172 milligrams of potassium, and 31 milligrams of calcium may be derived from this dish. We may deduce that a person is fed a significant amount of required nutrients, vital to maintaining a healthy, heart-friendly diet.

Dash's dietary followers will experience normal blood pressure in just 14 days, with fewer tendencies to eat intermediate meals, which is the main culprit for weight gain. The Dash Diet Program also enables people to assess the correct amount of food consumption and exercise required, according to age and activity level.

Dash educates and inspires, one of the most important reasons it is easy for people to adhere to their diet. Furthermore, the diet does not require us to give up something necessary for our daily diet, but it helps us build by adapting to little changes to support ourselves effectively.

The Dash diet is believed to prevent cardiovascular diseases, diabetes, and colon cancer. With its goal of instilling the lesson of salt in the common person's mind quickly, it has been able to help save more than 40% of people with hypertension lives.

Our foods affect our overall health. A diet rich in unhealthy factors such as saturated fats and cholesterol is a healthy way to treat high blood pressure and other diseases. A proper food option will decrease the risk of contracting these diseases.

The DASH diet is a clear diet that has been shown to reduce hypertension or elevated blood pressure. The diet is referred to as the DASH or nutritional strategy to avoid high blood pressure. The DASH diet is the product of research performed by researchers of the National Institute of Heart, Lung, and Blood (NHLBI). Researchers found that diets that are high in potassium, magnesium, calcium, protein, and fiber, and low in fat and cholesterol can reduce high blood pressure significantly.

Three essential nutrients are also stressed in the DASH diet: magnesium, calcium, and potassium. These minerals are intended to minimize high blood pressure. A standard 2,000-calorie diet includes 500 mg magnesium, 4.7 g potassium, and 1.2 g calcium. It is very easy to adopt the DASH diet and takes little time to pick and prepare meals. Foods high in cholesterol and fats are avoided. Dieters should eat, as much as possible, vegetables, fruit, and cereals.

Provided that the foods consumed in a DASH diet are high in fiber content, you can slowly raise your fiber-rich food intake to prevent diarrhea and other digestive problems. By consuming an additional portion of fruit and vegetables in each meal, you will gradually increase your fiber consumption.

Grains and B-complex vitamins and minerals are also healthy sources of fiber. Whole grain, pieces of bread, whole wheat bran, wheat germ, and low-fat breakfast cereals are some of the cereals you should eat to improve your fiber.

The food you consume can be picked by looking at the product labels of processed and packaged foods. Find low-fat, saturated fat, sodium, and cholesterol foods. The key sources of fat and cholesterol are meats, chocolates, chips, and fast foods, so you must reduce your foods intake.

If you wish to eat meat, limit your meal to just 6 oz. a day, close in size to a card deck. In your meat dishes, you can eat more fruits, cereals, pasta, and beans. Low-fat milk or skim milk is a significant protein source without excess fat and cholesterol.

For snacks, you should try both fresh and canned fruit. Safe snacks are also available for people on the DASH diet, such as unsalted nuts, graham crackers, and low-fat yogurt.

Among many health benefits, the DASH diet is popular because special foods and recipes are required. The DASH diet is a balanced eating plan that focuses more on the three main minerals expected to improve blood pressure concerns.

The DASH diet is perfect for people who want warmth and ease of food. The DASH diet provides a tried and tested nutritional framework of empirical evidence for those seeking good health.

You should consider using the DASH diet if you are already suffering from high blood pressure or hypertension. You will need to talk to your doctor before deciding if you want to start a DASH diet to ensure it is right for you. Your doctor may also help you make the right decisions to ensure that your DASH diet succeeds.

As previously stated, you should eat foods high in calcium, magnesium, and potassium to be effective in your diet. Examples of foods rich in these three nutrients are fruits, vegetables, nuts, and milk products with low-fat content. However, taking supplements instead of eating these foods won't help you reduce your high blood pressure. These nutrients must be consumed from natural foods.

You will probably want to increase your intake of whole-grain foods and reduce the amount of sodium in your diet, in addition to eating a lot of fruits and vegetables. Fish and poultry can also be included in your diet but it is best to consult your doctor to find out what is the right amount for you.

It can be a bit of a challenge, like beginning any other diet, but you will excel if you take baby steps rather than make a huge drastic shift. Many times, if you do all at once, you tend to miss the foods you enjoyed but couldn't have anymore, and you give up. You can make your diet a part of your everyday routine by doing it slowly.

The way to take baby steps is to include some of your regular meal diets and set your own goals. For example, you can purchase ready-made crust, add low-fat cheese, and add loads of nutrients such as broccoli, tomatoes, and spinach to your pizza. Or, instead of oily potato chips, you could have raw vegetables with lower-fat yogurt dip. As for setting targets, you can tell yourself that you plan to snack at least one fruit each day rather than cookies or sweets.

If you have high blood pressure, the DASH diet is probably worth doing. Be sure that you consult the doctor to see how you can do that and follow the doctor's instructions. Healthy eating and a good fitness schedule will help you minimize your high blood pressure.

How Dash Diet Works

This is the nutritional strategy to avoid and even treat high blood pressure. This diet has existed for the past 10 years now, and it works most of the time, according to a variety of accounts. In reality, a study shows you the results you are looking for after eight weeks of following this diet. The diet is tailored if you adopt it to reduce high blood pressure. The diet demands that you remain free from foodstuffs high in sodium.

This means you can skip the processed foods you usually purchase for your family. Various rules should also be followed if you incorporate DASH to control high blood pressure into your lifestyle. The diet also includes a reduction in total fat and saturated fat intake. If any of the foods that contain these cannot be avoided, you must restrict your fat intake.

Veggies and fruits are also popular in this diet and this high blood pressure management tool. The diet advises you that selected fruits and vegetables must be included in your diet. It is also recommended to get at least 8 to 10 portions of salads and vegetables high in potassium. Bananas are a great source of potassium and can be used in your diet.

It is also a rule in DASH that you are only serving low-fat dairy products correctly. Something excessive is also harmful to your body. Low-fat products are high in magnesium and calcium and eating 3 portions of these foods will help your body get the required dietary supplies of magnesium and calcium every day. For more specific food guidelines, see below some of the food products you need to consider to control high blood pressure. The foods to include in your diet are:

1. Beans, nuts, and poultry in their entirety.
2. Consume legumes and beans, too.
3. Stay away from processed food products such as frozen foods, tuna, and corned beef, and say no to junk and snack food.
4. As stated, fruit and vegetables rich in potassium must be included. The fruit guideline is up to 10 portions of fruit and veggies, and only 3 portions of low-fat dairy items should be included.

With these, it's easier for you to ensure that you have a balanced lifestyle and fun when you decide to control high blood pressure. The DASH diet is what you need as it advises you on foods that minimize blood pressure.

DASH Diet and Loss of Weight

With increased physical activity, you will lose weight when adopting the DASH diet plan at lower calorie amounts. The easiest way to lose weight is to gradually get more physical exercise and consume a healthy diet lower in calories and fat.

Physical exercise can be carried out for 30 minutes at the same time or for 3 different intervals of 10 minutes each. Try taking about 60 minutes a day overall to prevent weight gain.

To encourage weight loss, the DASH Eating Plan can be implemented. It is abundant in foods with lower calories, such as fruit and vegetables. You will reduce the number of calories by swapping higher-calorie foods like candy for more fruits and vegetables, making it easier for you to meet your DASH goals. Such instances are as follows:

1. Instead of four shortbread cookies, eat a medium apple. You're going to save 80 calories. Eat a fifth of a cup of dried apricots rather than a twin bag of pork rinds. You're going to save 230 calories.

2. Have a hamburger, 3 oz. of meat rather than 6 oz. Put a ½ cup of carrots and a ½ cup of spinach. You're going to save over 200 calories. Stir in 2 oz. of chicken and 1½ cups of raw vegetables instead of 5 oz. of chicken, using a little vegetable oil. You're going to save 50 calories.
3. Increasing fat-free or low-fat milk products; have ½ cup serving of frozen low-fat yogurt rather than ½ cup serving full of fat ice cream. You're going to save about 70 calories.

Other tips to save calories:

1. Use fat-free condiments. Use half as much soft margarine vegetable oil, liquid margarine, salad dressing, or mayonnaise, or select low-fat or fat-free options available. Eat smaller servings and eventually cut back.
2. Choose milk and dairy products: fat-free or low-fat. To compare the food labels of processed goods and products free of fat or reduced fat content, they are not necessarily lower in calories than normal versions. Limit foods with plenty of added sugar, such as pies, flavored yogurts, chocolate, ice cream, sherbet, daily fruit, and soft drinks.
3. Add fruit to plain low-fat or fat-free yogurt — fruit snacks, sticks of vegetables, popcorn, or rice cakes unbuttered and unsalted. Drink water or soda and zest with a lemon or lime slice.

Concept of the Dash Diet

The Dash diet is based on the following principles:

1. Reduction in salt consumption

One of the main goals of the Dash diet is to reduce the consumption of salt drastically.

Of course, man cannot live without salt. The human body contains around 150 to 300 grams of table salt. The amount of salt lost through sweating and other excretions must therefore be replaced. Salt supports bone structure and digestion. It maintains the osmotic pressure in the vessels to maintain the water and nutrient levels. But nowadays our foods are filled with a lot of salt — especially all finished products.

The extent to which increased salt consumption has a negative impact on health is currently the subject of intense discussion among experts, especially since the body excretes excess salt.

But studies from 1970 in Finland already show that too much salt causes blood pressure to skyrocket. It could be shown that the reduced consumption of salt by 30% could even reduce mortality from heart attacks by 80%.

A study on mice published in 2007 at the University Hospital in Heidelberg showed that a lot of salt increases blood pressure: "Salt promotes the formation of certain messenger substances in the muscles of blood vessels that cause the muscle cells to contract. The increased resistance in the blood vessels increases blood pressure." Therefore, the Heidelberg scientists, see considerable advantages in reducing the amount of salt in food compared to conventional drugs.

There is disagreement among scientists about how high the maximum amount of salt can be. While US experts recommend a maximum of 1.5 grams of salt per day, the German Nutrition Society's recommendation is 6 grams per day. The upper limit is 10 grams per day. 6 grams are roughly equivalent to an em tsp.

However, this only applies to a healthy person who moves sufficiently and is physically active and excretes the salt again through sweating. For example, an athlete can tolerate more salt than someone who only moves moderately.

I recommend that you only look at these values as a rough guide and begin to control your salt consumption and gradually reduce it. Also, keep in mind that the maximum amount of salt that you should consume depends on your body constitution and lifestyle.

Recommendation:

- Less is more! Therefore, pay more attention to your salt consumption in the future and reduce it step by step. The keyword is low-salt, but not salt-free!
- Avoid finished products (packaged food, pizza, French fries, chips, canned food, various meat and fish products, baked goods, etc.). If necessary, read the list of ingredients.

- If possible, use a natural salt substitute (herbs, etc.) in your meals
- Use low-water cooking methods such as stewing or steaming. This means that the food remains tastier, and you don't need to salt it as much.

2. More vitamin E and minerals

The Dash diet is based on a variety of fruits and vegetables and whole-grain products to provide the body with plenty of vitamins and minerals. Particular attention is paid to minerals such as magnesium and potassium, which help lower or improve blood pressure.

3. More healthy fats and oils

Fats are energy carriers and ensure that fat-soluble vitamins such as vitamins E, D, and K can be absorbed by the body completely. Certain fatty acids, such as omega-3 and omega-6 fatty acids, are also essential, which means that we can only get them from food. Therefore, they should be on a regular meal plan. The omega-6/3 ratio plays a vital role in health. Omega-3 fatty acids help to maintain normal blood pressure levels wisely. However, our diet often contains too few omega-3 fatty acids. Good sources of this are fatty fish such as herring, mackerel, salmon, and sardines.

This also applies to the use of oils. Z and healthy oils include virgin cold-pressed olive oil and coconut oil (in organic quality).

Unlike olive oil, coconut oil can also be heated and used for frying and baking. On the other hand, the much-used sunflower oil is less healthy because it only contains omega-6 fatty acids. This creates an imbalance in the omega-3 to omega-6 ratio. A ratio between 1: 2 and 1: 5 should be aimed for.

Ultimately, as with most other diets, the Dash diet should avoid unhealthy fats, especially trans fats, a subgroup of unsaturated fatty acids, and replace them with healthy fats such as those found in nuts, seeds, and fish. Trans fatty acids come from industrial production and are, for example, contained in chips, baked goods, French fries, confectionery, pizza, etc.

4. More fiber

Fiber is an integral part of the Dash diet. A fiber-rich diet, whether through fruits, vegetables, grains, and cereals, positively affects blood pressure and the cardiovascular system.

In contrast to the low-carb diet, grain can therefore be consumed. However, it is important to consume only wholesome grains (whole grain bread).

5. Egg whites/proteins

Proteins are an important part of the Dash diet and should be consumed in beans, lentils, fish, and soy products.

6. White instead of dark meat

Animal fat should be avoided as far as possible. It is high in cholesterol and saturated fat. Therefore, red meat should be avoided entirely if possible. Instead, white meat (chicken, turkey) can be put on the plate.

7. Avoid butter

Even if opinions differ widely about butter consumption, especially about its effect on the cholesterol level, the Dash diet specifies that butter should be avoided as far as possible. Therefore, butter no longer belongs in the refrigerator. Vegetable oils should serve as a substitute.

Now margarine is anything but healthy and therefore not an alternative in my opinion. Therefore, recommend switching to ghee, the Ayurvedic butter. Ghee is pure butterfat and contains 70% saturated fatty acids. In Ayurveda, Ghee has been used for healing purposes for thousands of years. Studies have shown that ghee can even lower cholesterol and prevent diseases such as cardiovascular diseases. The advantage of ghee is that, unlike butter, it can be heated to a high temperature.

8. Low-fat dairy products

The reduced-fat variant should always be preferred for dairy products (max. 1.5% fat content).

9. Less alcohol, caffeine, and nicotine

Alcohol increases blood pressure. The Dash diet recommends avoiding alcohol, beverages containing caffeine, and nicotine as much as possible to reduce blood pressure.

If you don't want to go without your coffee, you should enjoy it with as little or no sugar as possible.

It is also known that smoking increases the risk of heart attacks and strokes. So, if you haven't already done so, put an end to the glowing stick!

10. Reduction of industrial sugar (granulated sugar)

Most people should know by now that too much sugar is not healthy. The Dash diet does not completely exclude sugar. After all, fresh and dried fruits are an important part of this diet, and of course, they also contain sugar (fructose).

What has a negative effect on blood pressure, however, is pure industrial sugar. This can quickly increase blood pressure and should be avoided as far as possible. The best way to regulate daily sugar consumption is to avoid sweets and finished products.

A possible alternative to industrial sugar, which is not exactly cheap, is coconut blossom sugar, which, despite its calories, keeps the blood sugar level more constant.

11. Check daily calorie intake

The Dash diet recommends a calorie intake between 1,500 and 2,300 kcal per day. If you want to lose weight, you should limit the value to 1,500 kcal per day. Of course, this is only a guideline and depends on the basal metabolic rate, age, body weight and size, muscular mass, gender, and health status. You can find a variety of calculators on the Internet to determine your calorie requirement (e.g., with Fit-for-Fun, Smart Calculator).

Beginning the DASH Diet

Now that you are supplied with the necessary background information on the DASH diet, let us see first what it entails. This meal plan is rich in vegetables, fruits, dairy products, whole grains, lean meats, poultry, fish, and legumes such as peas and beans. Additionally, it contains low fat from natural sources and high fiber from sweet potatoes, cabbage, and leafy vegetables. It adheres to the US guidelines about sodium and potassium content. It is a flexible eating plan designed to meet the needs of a variety of people keeping in mind their food preferences. There is a healthy alternative to almost any kind of food craving. It is what a typical DASH diet comprises:

Type of Food	Number of servings (1600–3000 calorie plan)	Number of servings (1500–2000 calorie plan)
Whole grains or meals made out of whole grains	6–12	7–9
Fresh fruits (not fruit juice)	4–5	4–6
Farm fresh vegetables (try avoiding store-bought ones)	4–6	4–6
Dairy products (low fat)	3–4	2–4
Poultry, fish, lean meats	2–3	3–4
Legumes, seeds, and nuts	3–5	4–5
Desserts, natural fats	2–3	2

Does It Work for Everyone?

Many people may benefit from the DASH diet, but even so, the best results were seen in individuals that already have high blood pressure. With that in mind, if your blood pressure is within normal levels, the chances are that you may not see any significant results.

Some doctors also suggest that several categories of people should exercise caution when undergoing the DASH diet. While the diet is safe and healthy for most people, those who have chronic liver disease, kidney disease, or those who have been prescribed renin-angiotensin-aldosterone system (RAAS) inhibitors should be careful. Ideally, discussions with your physician should be due.

Certain modifications of the DASH diet may also be necessary in case the person has chronic heart failure, lactose intolerance, Mellitus type 2, and celiac disease. This is why you may want to keep in touch with your healthcare provider to be certain that the diet is your best choice. Depending on the circumstances, you may as well need to make some modifications to the diet.

Chapter 2

The Main Benefits of the Dash Diet

Although you're likely to go for the DASH diet because of a slimmer waist and better health, there are more reasons to consider the DASH diet. They include the following:

Controlled Blood Pressure

This is the main benefit of the DASH diet and the reason why nutritionists and physicians recommend it. Following DASH lets you keep your blood pressure in check. This diet is ideal for anyone who is taking medication to control blood pressure and those with prehypertension symptoms and are looking for better ways of managing these symptoms. DASH is specially designed to help tame blood pressure and has been scientifically proven to work.

Healthy Eating

Let's face it. One of the reasons why most people experience high blood pressure is because of being overweight or obese, which is associated with poor eating choices. Following the DASH diet helps you make a lifestyle change to healthy eating. Thus, you will be spending more time in the kitchen preparing fresh food as opposed to grabbing processed food on the go. You will also enjoy your meal times because your plate will be filled with foods that are more nutritious. DASH also stretches you a little to try out new vegetables and fruits and experiment with various seasonings that are salt-free to create meals that you will enjoy.

Reduced Risk of Osteoporosis

The majority of dietary approaches to prevent and treat osteoporosis include increasing your intake of calcium and vitamin D that is found in abundance in foods that are recommended for the DASH diet. This coupled with a reduced intake of sodium is proof that the DASH diet is quite beneficial for bone health. Some studies found a notable decline in bone turnover for people who followed the DASH diet. When sustained over a longer period, the DASH diet is instrumental in improving bone mineral status. Other nutrients that are in abundance in the DASH diet and are excellent at promoting bone health over time include vitamin C, antioxidants, magnesium, and polyphenols.

Healthy Cholesterol Levels

Since most of the fruits, beans, nuts, whole grains, and vegetables that are recommended under the DASH diet have high fiber content, you can eat them alongside fish and lean meat while limiting your intake of refined carbohydrates and sweets. This goes a long way in improving your cholesterol levels.

Better Weight Management

The DASH diet is a perfect option when you want to maintain a healthy weight or are keen on losing weight. You can follow a version of the DASH diet that is tailored to help you achieve weight loss goals after which you can stick to a higher calorie count in order to maintain your ideal weight. This means you won't have to worry about gaining weight again. The DASH diet provides an abundance of proteins without including too many carbohydrates. Thus, you will be able to build muscle as well as boost your metabolism without feeling heavy. Even better, this is not a short-term change but a lifestyle.

Healthier Kidneys

The DASH diet lowers the risk for kidney stones and kidney disease because of the abundance of magnesium, potassium, calcium, and fiber present in the foods encouraged. The focus on reducing sodium intake is also an advantage if you face the risk of developing kidney disease. Even then, the DASH diet should be restricted to patients who have chronic kidney disease, as well as those undergoing dialysis without the close guidance of professional qualified health care.

Easy to Maintain

The DASH diet is designed around foods that are readily available, which makes it easier to follow and maintain. Apart from comprising foods that leave you feeling satiated for most of the day, you can eat two or three snacks per day. When you commit to this diet, you can be sure to enjoy long-term changes in your lifestyle that are a plus for your overall wellness and health. You can even follow the DASH diet even when you're eating out at a restaurant because all you need to do is beware of those foods that are likely to jeopardize your efforts. Besides, there are many ways of making this diet work for you.

Prevents Diabetes

The DASH diet is effective in the prevention of insulin resistance that has been linked to cardiovascular risks and high blood pressure. By managing your sodium intake, maintaining a healthy weight, as well as eating more potassium and fiber, this eating plan helps delay or prevent the onset of diabetes if you are predisposed to the disease. Studies have further shown that the impact is even better when you implement the DASH diet as a component of a comprehensive healthy lifestyle that includes exercise, diet, and weight control.

Decreased Risk of Certain Cancers

Researchers have studied the relationship between the DASH diet and certain types of cancers and found a positive association that relates to reducing salt intake and monitoring consumption of dietary fat. The diet is also low in red meat which is linked to cancer of the rectum, colon, esophagus, lung, stomach, kidney, and prostate. Eating plenty of fresh produce is helpful in preventing various cancers while emphasizing dairy products that are low in fat contributes to a drop in the risk of colon cancer.

Better Mental Health

The DASH diet will boost your mood while decreasing symptoms of mental health disorders like anxiety or depression. This is associated with various lifestyle changes that include avoiding cigarettes, moderating alcohol consumption and exercising regularly. Moreover, the inclusion of nutrient-rich foods in the diet also helps in balancing out hormones and chemicals in the brain and body, thus contributing to improved mental health and overall well-being.

You Feel Less Hungry

By consuming high protein and high fiber foods, the DASH diet will leave no room for cravings for fast foods. Instead, you tend to feel more satiated throughout the day and only look forward to the next nutritious and filling meal. However, you can always identify some DASH-friendly snacks just in case you feel you need to snack. Cutting on carbs and eating low-fat diets can leave you feeling restricted and hungry; however, the DASH diet is easier to stick to because it keeps you satisfied.

Healthy Lifestyle

The DASH plan is more than the diet; it's more about being able to take control of your health and wellness in ways that are manageable. Thus, by balancing between healthy living, exercise, and nutrition, you can be sure to see a wider range of valuable benefits in addition to the wellness that you will experience with the DASH diet plan.

Anti-Aging Properties

Many people who follow the DASH diet have attested to the fact that this diet helps in avoiding some effects of aging so that they keep them feeling and looking younger. Increasing your consumption of fresh vegetables and fruits that are full of antioxidants will rejuvenate your hair and skin, revitalize and strengthen your joints, muscles, and bones, help you lose weight, and leave you feeling healthier.

Improved Cognitive Function

According to research, the DASH diet will help keep your brain sharp and avoid memory loss, thus significantly slowing your mental decline rate. Besides, high fiber and low-fat eating can promote lower blood pressure which is usually a risk factor in the development of degenerative conditions like dementia and Alzheimer's disease. Some of the best foods that are helpful in curbing mental decline that is included in the DASH diet include whole grains, vegetables, low-fat dairy, legumes, and nuts.

Reduced Risk of Developing Heart Disease

The ability of the DASH diet to keep your blood pressure in check is instrumental in strengthening the body's resistance to heart disease. According to a 2010 study, DASH has the ability to substantially lower the risk of heart disease. This is particularly great given the persistent and enormous burden of coronary heart disease. This finding is attributed to the fact that lowered blood pressure lets the heart function efficiently and effectively. Moreover, it can also be beneficial for those who are not struggling with hypertension but are keen on preventing the onset of heart disease.

Chapter 3

Why Is Important to Follow the Dash Diet, and How Is Possible to Have Tasty and Healthy Food

DASH is one of the simplest diets to follow. Since it is unrestrictive in calories, there is no need to count them. There is simply to learn what foods are available on the diet, and how many times per day or week you can have them. Most of the foods, such as fruits and vegetables, can be eaten at every meal and in ample portions.

Since DASH foods are the type of foods that can be found anywhere and are not 'special' foods for a specific diet, DASH dieters can eat out when they want to if they simply follow the guidelines. This is quite the opposite of most other diets that make it difficult to eat out in a restaurant. DASH dieting does not keep you from being able to enjoy going out to a friend or family's house to eat, or a potluck supper, or even a banquet. It only requires that you avoid the foods that are not allowed on the diet, or keep those types of foods to a minimum.

Going on the DASH diet means that you get to enjoy fresh, whole, delicious foods, prepared in the ways that are the most healthful for your body. There will be some small changes in the way that some of the foods are prepared, for example, meat, fish, or poultry may be broiled instead of fried. Dessert may consist of low-fat frozen yogurt instead of ice cream. Most of the changes are so slight as to not be noticeable or are easily accommodated

IS THE DASH DIET A FAD?

The DASH diet is definitely not a fad, and it is not going anywhere anytime soon. DASH has been so well received around the world for its real-life success stories of people from all walks of life changing their eating habits and adopting DASH.

Many 'fad' diets have come and gone through the years. Some of them even re-emerge from time to time, but the thing that separates a fad diet from a healthy way of eating is that fads do not deliver on their claims and they are short-lived in the lives of the people who are on them.

An example of a fad diet is the Adkins diet, which restricts carbohydrate intake and initially helps dieters to lose weight, often a substantial amount of weight. The real problem comes when the dieter goes off of the diet and begins to consume carbs again. You can guess what happens — the dieter gains back all of the weight, plus some additional weight. The reason almost all dieters gain back more weight than they originally lose is due to the brain's reactive mechanism, which rationally talks to the body and tells it that it has done without such for a long enough time, and it won't do any harm to have it now. This is the trip-up to almost all dieters who go off of their diet. If you have starved the body of carbs for 6 months, and can suddenly have them, along with everything else you would like to have, weight is going to come back.

There are very few dieters who are able to keep the weight off after it's been lost. This is what makes these diets a fad. They come and go, and often after they've been gone for a while, they resurface and gain popularity again for a while. Yet, the word of mouth that at first makes the diet gain momentum is not sufficient in results to keep the propulsion going. Since the diet does not work, the fad fizzles out.

DASH is not a fad for two main reasons. First, it delivers on the claims that it works. Second, it doesn't starve your body of anything that would trigger the reactive mechanism trying to trick your body into indulging. The body is constantly content on DASH, satisfied with the amount and the types of foods that it is allowed to enjoy.

That word 'enjoy' leads us to another element of DASH. DASH dieters actually enjoy the food that is available for them to eat during the day. Unlike other diets that require the dieter to eat specialized foods, such as plain toast with nothing on it, or a poached egg with no accompaniment. Many diets cause the dieter to feel trapped or imprisoned within the confines of the rules. DASH breaks out of those rules and puts all the control in the hands of the dieter.

How Will You Feel on the DASH Diet?

The DASH diet makes you feel superior to almost any other way of eating. This is not just a weak claim that DASH makes, it is scientifically proven that people who eat the kinds of foods that are recommended on DASH will feel great, lose weight, and not be hungry during the day. DASH fills you up with high-nutrient plant-based foods, lean meats, and whole grains, which keep you fueled between meals, keep your mind alert, and most importantly, build your body instead of draining it by calorie restriction.

After you ditch all of the junk food in your pantry and begin shopping for DASH foods, you will notice that when the junk foods are out of sight, they really are out of mind. When you're hungry and go looking for something to eat, and there is a wide range of healthy snacks to choose from, you're going to make a better choice because DASH foods are delicious and they are good for you. Shopping for, and eating, DASH food becomes second nature before long. Even when you're away from home, it becomes natural to make better choices from the available foods.

It's no secret that to feel good you have to put good food into your body. The DASH diet incorporates the kinds of foods that are important to maintain good nutrition and a healthy weight.

WHAT ARE THE SUCCESS RATES OF DASH DIETERS?

The DASH diet success rates are measured in two parts. First, the percentage of DASH dieters who liked the diet while on it, and second, the percentage of dieters who lost weight and kept it off. In both groups of people, percentages were higher than almost all other diets on the mainstream market. The contributing factor to the high percentage of people who stay on the diet, lose weight, and keep it off is related to the first factor, being that most people on the diet actually like the food. The two contributing factors go hand in hand.

When dieters feel imprisoned by the slim choices of foods that they are allowed to eat while on a particular diet, it greatly reduces the success of the diet itself, meaning dieters who don't enjoy the food will not stay on the diet. On the contrary, dieters who feel liberated by the range of 'allowed' foods on a food plan are much more apt to continue with the plan, as it does not impose on their normal way of life.

Another huge contributor to keeping a dieter on a diet is whether or not the types of foods on the diet are readily available when the dieter is away from home. Many diets limit the dieter's ability to eat out, a huge factor involved when considering staying on a diet or abandoning it. DASH dieters find that they can go out to many casual or fine dining experiences without having to worry about bringing food from home to eat while other members of their dining party are ordering off of the menu.

To sum all of that up, DASH dieters have huge success rates, especially compared to other diets. Many people who decide to add the DASH plan to their lives discover that they never want to go off of it. Once you discover how good you feel when on the DASH diet, you may decide to stay on it for a lifetime, as other people do.

7 Ways to Make Food Tasty Without Salt

1. <u>Avoid ready meals</u>

Ready meals are so convenient, and it's easier to order a pizza than to cook it yourself. But do check the nutritional information on the ready meals you buy to reheat at home or to put in the microwave.

Most of these items are loaded with sodium, chemicals, and additives. What are the solutions? Try quick, semi-homemade side dishes. Here are some of my favorites:

<u>15-Minute Roasted Broccoli</u>: Mix pre-cut broccoli florets with olive oil, garlic, and a pinch of salt (yes, that's right) and bake in a hot oven for 12 to 15 minutes.

<u>Sodium savings</u>: compared to frozen broccoli in cheese or butter sauce per cup = 420 mg

<u>Homemade sweet potatoes</u>: Bake in the oven or microwave, or (for those who think ahead) put them in the slow cooker in the morning to make

delicious sweet potatoes for dinner. Garnish with a little butter, a little salt, and your favorite spices.

Sodium savings: compared to chilled mashed potatoes or frozen French fries per serving = 730 mg

You can also use green beans, fruit salad, baby carrots with 2 Tbsps of hummus, or just about any product, fresh or frozen, as natural as possible.

Sodium savings: usually 300 to 800 mg sodium per side dish.

2. **Choose your canned food carefully**

For example, there are some cans that I can't do without: black beans and diced tomatoes.

However, canned foods usually require preservatives, which means that the sodium content is always higher. However, there are a few tricks you can use to reduce the sodium content when using them.

For items like beans, simply drain and rinse before use. This can reduce up to 40% of the sodium. When I checked the doses in my own pantry, it meant washing away 200 mg of sodium per ½ cup.

A second way to get around sodium is to look for products called "reduced salt" or "salt-free." Usually, you add canned food to something else — a dish or recipe that needs to be seasoned.

With other spices and flavors, the state of the dish hardly changes and 50 to 80% of the sodium is saved compared to regular versions.

Sodium savings: approx. 100 to 400 mg sodium per ½ cup of beans and 150 to 300 mg per ½ cup of canned tomatoes

3. **Cook chicken more often**

Chicken breasts are a staple of many family meals because of their versatility, kid-friendliness, and reputation for being a "healthy" choice. But they can add extra sodium to your plate.

What many people are unaware of is that raw chicken breast fillets are often injected with a saline solution to increase juiciness and add weight. This process uses a low-sodium food and adds four to five times normal sodium levels — before adding any more spices.

Since January 2016, manufacturers have had to indicate the percentage by weight that an injected solution makes up for raw poultry and most types of meat.

Obviously, buying chicken with no solution is best, but these are hard to find. Your next best attempt is to find breast meat with about 1 to 2% added solution — the lower the better. Also note that "solution" equates to adding sodium, whether it's salt and water, or healthy-sounding broth and spices.

<u>Sodium savings:</u> up to 400 mg sodium per chicken breast.

4. <u>Fresh salads and homemade dressings</u>

Increasing the intake of fresh products is an essential part of a heart-healthy diet. Fresh vegetables are naturally low in sodium and have a higher potassium content.

It is easier to prepare fresh salads.

But be careful, pre-made salad dressings are usually loaded with sodium.

Fortunately, salad dressing is very easy to make. It takes about 3 minutes to combine the ingredients in a mason jar and you will reduce sodium significantly. Just try a couple of vinaigrettes. Don't be afraid to experiment!

<u>Sodium savings:</u> 150 to 400 mg per 2 Tbsps.

5. <u>Freeze these leftovers</u>

Research has shown that home-cooked meals almost always contain fewer calories and fewer saturated fat and sodium than foods cooked "away" (i.e. fast food and restaurant dishes, but also pre-made products that you reheat at home, such as frozen pizzas or French fries Fries).

However, let's face it, there will be a few times when you have no other option but to warm up something. In this case, the convenience of having your own "frozen dinners" on hand and not having to order pizza or pasta.

The easiest way is to double or triple the amounts of ingredients in a favorite recipe — for example in a casserole or soup. Serve for dinner and freeze the extras in 2 to 4 servings. You save a lot of sodium — and money too, of course!

Sodium savings: 900 mg for a serving of chicken broccoli casserole to 1800 mg for a plate of chicken tortilla soup.

6. Swap your snacks

For many people, a "snack" usually means high levels of carbohydrates that are sweet, salty, or both.

Packaged snacks are very convenient (and often just a vending machine away), but a few salty snacks can add extra sodium throughout the day.

Swap them out for fresh fruit, yogurt, roasted chickpeas, or raw vegetables with a little hummus — all with a little less sodium.

Sodium savings: approx. 100 to 250 mg sodium depending on the exchange.

7. Balance in your sodium account

When tracking your sodium intake throughout the day, it is difficult to ignore how much you are consuming and the positive and negative effects of the various food options. Hence, from time to time it is good to keep track of your "sodium account" just like you would with a checking account.

In the morning, write 2300 mg on a piece of paper or on a virtual sticky note on your smartphone. Then use the nutrition facts to subtract your sodium deficits later in the day. You will get a good feel for how well (or badly) you can stay in positive territory.

I've found that with this regularly heightened awareness, I can make better decisions, even on days when I'm not tracking my sodium consumption.

And when I tracked my sodium intake for three days, I found that I could get it down to 1,100 to 1,850 mg on foods I normally consumed, just by simply comparing nutritional information and making smarter sodium choices.

Chapter 4.

What to Eat and Avoid

Now that we know what the DASH diet is, the benefits of the diet, and a brief overview of what nutrients are lowered and increased in consumption under the DASH diet, let's talk about what foods you can eat on the diet and what should be avoided. We will also look at portion sizes for healthy DASH diet meals throughout the day. Remember, the DASH diet is a lifelong change, so don't constrict your diet, only change it.

Good Foods to Eat

To start, *grains* are essential in the dash diet. This can include pasta, rice, cereal, and bread. Grains are the main servings of your diet, meaning you should consume around 6–8. This varies depending on the person, but for an average 2,000 calorie diet, this is a suitable amount of servings. One serving can come in the form of a slice of whole-wheat bread, half a cup of cooked pasta or rice, or one oz. of dry cereal.

The next largest food group is *vegetables*. For the average 2,000 calorie diet, 4–5 servings of vegetables should be eaten throughout the day. Fiber and vitamin-rich vegetables are great for the DASH diet.

Fruits. Fruits are important to the DASH diet because they are high in fiber, potassium, magnesium, and other vital vitamins and minerals. A wide variety of fruits can be eaten and to up the amount of fiber you eat, don't peel the skin off some of your favorite fruits, such as apples. The skin is packed with fiber nutrients.

Nuts, seeds, and legumes should be also consumed on par with fruits and vegetables. Strive to have 4–5 servings a day of these super-packed nutritional foods. They provide protein, potassium, magnesium, fiber, phytochemicals, and other nutrients. Various beans, seeds, and nuts can be added to your diet to achieve these serving goals.

Low-fat or fat-free dairy products should make up only 2–3 servings of your daily nutritional intake. This can include milk, cheese, or yogurt. When buying these items, we stress the fact that they should be low or fat-free. Dairy is placed in the DASH diet for a boost in calcium, protein, and vitamin D, not for a boost in calories and fat.

Poultry and fish are allowed on the DASH diet, with a maximum of 6 one-oz. servings a day. However, you should try to aim to eat mainly vegetables and replace what would be meat in your food with vegetables. If you do choose to eat meat, avoid seasoning with salt and remove the skin before eating. When eating fish, go for fish that are high in omega-3 fatty acids. This can be fish like salmon as they are great for heart health, a staple of the DASH diet.

Fats and oils should have only 2–3 servings a day. A little bit of fat is necessary as it helps your body absorb vitamins and boost your immune system. However, too much fat counteracts the DASH diet by raising the risks for diseases like heart attacks and disease. Healthier monosaturated fats are recommended by the DASH diet as they are better for you than fats found in processed foods. A serving of oil or fat can be 2 Tbsps of salad dressing or one Tbsp of mayonnaise. Everything is good in moderation. Remember this as you follow the DASH diet.

Sweets are not a staple of the DASH diet. It's recommended to have sweets 5 servings or fewer a week. Again, the DASH diet is not about restricting yourself from foods you crave but instead eating them in moderation. This is why the DASH diet allows you to have these "cheat" foods at small moderations throughout the week.

Alcohol. It's recommended that for women, no more than one drink a day should be consumed, and for men, no more than two per day. The best bet is to quit alcohol completely, but we understand that a drink every now and then is fine.

Bad Foods Not to Eat

Red meat should be avoided or eaten very rarely with the DASH diet. Red meat is high in fat and sodium content, which are both bad for your DASH diet. If you're craving meat, stick with poultry or lean pork.

Full-fat dairy products like heavy whipping cream or 2% milk should be avoided. This ups the servings of fat you're having in a day, and in order to stay on the DASH diet, you need to make your servings conscientiously count.

Fast food should be avoided because it is often high in sodium because of the processing of the food. This includes chips, pizza, and other unhealthy snacks. They can also hide secret sugars put in to make the food taste better, but the healthy nutrients decline.

The DASH diet is about purposeful eating. You are responsible for choosing foods that fuel you and give you energy, rather than tear you down. We will offer a wide variety of recipes later in this book, but for now, keep in mind these portion sizes and food groups when preparing your next meal on the DASH diet plan.

Chapter 5.

Dash Diet and Lifestyle

Change is hard. Whenever you make any type of change to your diet, especially if your goal is the development of lifelong, healthy habits, you will find that along the way, you will need some encouragement, advice, and strategy to help you get started, and also get through the rough spots that are inevitable. From navigating the grocery store to dealing with social circumstances, here are a few tips that will help you attain DASH Diet success.

You can't start on a new path without an awareness of where you have been, or you run the risk of going backward. The best way to begin the DASH Diet, or really any eating plan, is to take an honest look at your current eating habits. Use a food journal and record everything you eat and drink for several days. Take it a step further and analyze vital nutritional content, including sodium intake. This will give you a clean look at how you need to modify your current way of eating to be in line with DASH guidelines.

Don't do everything at once. Major changes take time, and if you keep this in mind, you are more likely to be successful with your new dietary lifestyle. Begin by making one or two small changes at a time, and keep with them until they begin to feel natural, before making more changes. For example, switch to lower fat dairy this week and work on adding more produce next week. Gradually increase servings of those fresh fruits and vegetables by adding on serving to one meal a day, for example. Not only will making these changes gradually be good for your mental commitment, but it will also help your body adjust to the increase in fiber and the slight detoxification you get from eliminating processed foods and extra sodium.

Familiarize yourself with portion sizes. So, you know that 1 serving of meat is 3 to 4 oz. and that you need to consume 4 to 5 servings of vegetables, but do you really understand what that looks like, and how consuming those amounts of foods will make you feel in terms of satiety? Understanding what portion sizes look and feel like will go a long way in helping you follow DASH Diet guidelines.

Don't be afraid to ask questions when you are dining out or enjoying dinners and parties at a friend's house. Ask how foods are prepared and what ingredients they contain. If you plan on doing DASH for life, there will likely be an occasion here or there where you just let the plan slide; however, if you live a lifestyle that has you frequently involved in entertaining or eating out, you need to step up and ask these questions to eliminate the risk of sabotaging your diet. If you are not comfortable letting your host know of your dietary restrictions, then offer to bring a dish or two to pass around. This will ensure that you also have something to enjoy and do not inconvenience anyone.

Beware of condiments and sauces as these are often heavy in salt, sugar, and fats. Even the most unassuming ones — such as ketchup — can add milligrams of salt and unwanted sugar to your diet. Ask for foods to be prepared without extra sauces or have them served on the side so that you are in charge of how much you consume.

Accept that you are human. DASH can be a lifelong approach to healthy eating and wellness protection as long as you are realistic about your expectations. There is room for moderation in this dietary plan; the main focus should not be on sacrifice, but on making healthy choices most of the time. Allow yourself an occasional treat, your mind and body will both thank you for it.

If your finances allow, invest in some good quality cookware and kitchen utensils. The right cookware will make preparing DASH meals easier, less messy, and they will taste better also. Think about non-stick cookware that eliminates the need for excess cooking oils, vegetable steamers, and rice cookers to make preparation effortless, and good quality spice mills for all of the flavorful and exotic new spices you will be experimenting with as you change your priorities from salty to flavorful.

Always read labels. Always. Pay particular attention to saturated fat, sodium, and fiber content. When something appears to be high in sodium or fats, weigh what you will be giving up against what you gain from one portion of that food and ask yourself if it is worth it. In some cases, you may feel that it is. In others, the idea of giving up several servings of other foods for just one of this food will be enough to persuade you to put it down and move on to something else.

Don't be afraid to modify your recipes. DASH isn't about putting your favorites away forever; it is about modifying them so that you can still enjoy them whenever you want without worrying that you are damaging your health. Make lower fat substitutions, reduce the amount of meat while increasing the amount of grains or vegetables, and reduce the amount of sugar and salt while making ingredient choices that enhance the flavor. For instance, add sugar-free applesauce to reduce the sugar content in a muffin recipe, or a nice spice blend to help you forget that you hardly used any salt in your treasured stew recipe.

Look at new ways of preparing foods. If you love fried foods, you can try oven frying those foods using olive oil and whole-wheat breading. Consider using low sodium broth instead of heavy oils for sautéing and learn how to steam, bake, and sauté your favorite foods. These preparations are not only healthier; they are easy and require little clean-up.

Never allow yourself to go hungry because when you are hungry you are more likely to indulge in the very foods you are trying to cut out of your life. If you find that you are hungry immediately after a meal, then your portions are too small, and you should bulk up your meals a little bit. Keep plenty of fresh snacks available to help curb hunger between meals.

Drink plenty of water. Make sure to get in at least 8–10 glasses per day.

Never go to the grocery store hungry. Either do your grocery shopping after a meal or keep a healthy snack (such as fruit or vegetables) in your car to nibble before you go in. If you are not hungry, you are more likely to stick with your dietary plan rather than splurging on things that provide you with no nutrition and too much salt and fat.

Discover the art of meal planning. There are two schools of thought on meal planning. Some people love it and enjoy devoting time to it. The other school of thought centers around the idea that it is just too much work and never works out anyway. I am here to tell you that there actually is a happy medium between these two. Even if you are not a fan of meal planning, start by planning half of your meals, even if it is just breakfast or lunch. Write out a menu, and what ingredients you need. Maybe a weekly meal plan for breakfast will only include oatmeal, eggs, low-fat yogurt, fresh berries, and asparagus. But you will know each day what you will be having, which helps you commit to actually giving yourself time for preparation and you will also know that you have everything you need for each of those meals. Start small and build on it. Soon, you will find that meal planning not only makes grocery shopping easier and is gentler on the wallet, but you will begin to look forward to certain meals throughout the week. This will also help you stay on track with your diet. If you are unsure of where to start with meal planning, there are several apps and websites that are helpful in creating simple weekly meal plans.

Choose fresh whenever possible. When fresh produce is an option, choose it over canned. Frozen produce is also an excellent option as there is not the same sodium content as in canned goods. Speaking of frozen foods, limit your choices to frozen vegetables and fruits while staying away from frozen prepared meals and snacks. If you are really craving those frozen jalapeno poppers, make your own by stuffing fresh peppers with low-fat cheese and spices. There is a healthy alternative to just about everything; there is no need to depend on the frozen food section for your favorite snacks and meals.

Make it from scratch. When you make your own sauces, salad dressings, and soups you are ensuring that your food contains natural, fresh ingredients with sodium and fat content that is much less than what you will find in their prepackaged counterparts.

If you do choose canned goods, rinse off the contents whenever possible. This especially applies to canned vegetables and meats.

Learn to shop the perimeter of the store. This is where you will find the foods that are promoted on the DASH Diet plan. Along the perimeter or outside aisles of your grocery store, you will find fresh produce, meat, seafood, dairy, and possibly a bakery where you can purchase fresh whole-grain bread. Save the middle aisles for things such as additional grains and spices only.

Flavor isn't just about the spice aisle. Yes, we make the point repeatedly about choosing other spices over salt. But you should also consider other foods that add incredible flavor to your dishes, like onion, garlic, fresh ginger, citrus, vinegar, and low sodium sauces.

Have a support system. Even better, have a multi-leveled support system. Get your family and friends involved in your decision and ask someone to be your accountability partner. These are the people that you will go to in times when you have difficulty sticking to the plan. We all start out with pure intentions, but when we are honest with ourselves, we know there will be times when we need a little nudge to stay on track. This is what your support is for. Also, it is helpful to have a medical support system that includes a physician or dietician that can help you along the way as you encounter questions or require evaluation.

Finally, reward yourself for a job well done, and forgive yourself when things don't go as planned. What are the things you dreamed about doing or accomplishing once you became healthier or lost some weight? Was it a new outfit, the confidence to finally join that group fitness class, run a half marathon, or take that spa trip with friends that you always found a way to talk yourself out of? These are the types of things you should reward yourself with as you reach your personal goals. But also, be gentle with yourself. You are setting out on a new road, and along the way, there will be bumps and you may feel shaken enough to jump off the path. You are more likely to stay true to your goals when you allow yourself to make a few mistakes. The process of changing your lifestyle is long-term, and it is an ongoing learning adventure. When you have a slip-up, evaluate what caused it and learn from your mistake. Forgive yourself, dust yourself off, and carry on. This is the path to success.

Exercise

Increasing how much physical activity you do is an extremely important part of any weight-loss program. It is essential for several health reasons.

Burns calories. Physical activity is fundamental to the Dash Diet for Weight Loss because it burns calories.

Boosts metabolism: The more muscle in our anatomies, the faster our metabolism, therefore, the more calories we burn. Once we grow old, we naturally begin to lose muscle tissue, which in turn causes our metabolism to decelerate.

A vicious cycle occurs. The less muscle we have, the slower our metabolism is, and the slower our metabolism, the more likely it is that we will gain weight. Physical activity is the key to breaking this cycle. Regular physical activity means you build muscle, which in turn means your metabolism will speed up. The beauty of this is that more muscle speeds up our metabolism even when we are at rest, not just when we are working out.

Increases strength. It is crucial to maintain muscle strength. Even if we do not need strength to do a lot of heavy work, having strong muscles allows us to do even routine daily activities more easily. It also helps us avoid injuries.

Improved Fitness Means Better Health. Being physically fit is good for you. Most of us know that. Sometimes, it is surprising to learn just how good it is for us. Exercise is so powerful that people who start exercising improve their health even if they do not lose any weight.

Exercise

- Reduces the threat of cardiovascular disease and stroke;
- Reduces the danger of developing diabetes;
- Reduces the risk of some types of cancer;
- Improves sexual function;
- Increases your possibility of living longer;
- Improves your mood.

Walking

Walking has many health advantages and is a minimal impact on aerobic fitness exercise. Of most types of exercise, walking may be the simplest, lowest, and most basic one. Everybody knows how to walk, and walking requires no specialized training or specific gear.

There are benefits of walking:

- Lowering cholesterol
- Lowering blood pressure
- Losing weight
- Reducing the threat of diabetes
- Restricting a depressed mood
- Increasing strength.

Walking is not an exercise with a lot of a threat of injury; however, when getting into any new workout program, it is important to take it easy in your body. Do not intend to walk five miles if you are just getting started. Be realistic. Focus on one mile or less for the first few tries, and slowly boost your distance and speed as the body becomes strong.

A very important thing about walking is that it is free. You can do it outside your entryway. It is wonderful to hear your preferred music, an audiobook, or even a motivational program while walking. The new air and visual impressions are great for the soul.

Additional low impact aerobic fitness exercise

When it is too cold to walk, you can find other light aerobic fitness exercise options that you could take part in. You might desire to buy a tai chi exercise video or join a program at your local community center.

There are other light aerobic exercise programs and activities such as cardio step exercise, stationary bicycling, or walking on a treadmill.

These activities might have a cost involved and a small learning curve, but they are low impact and carry the same health benefits as walking. It is essential always to wear proper footwear when doing any exercise program and to stay adequately hydrated.

Yoga

Yoga includes a note aerobic fitness exercise which has many health advantages, such as:

- Increased flexibility
- Increased strength
- Balanced mood
- Lower blood pressure
- Weight management
- Reduced stress
- Increased concentration
- Reduced insomnia
- Increased cardiovascular capacity.

It's important to understand yoga from a trained yoga instructor. Yoga is normally a minimal impact exercise; nonetheless, it does have certain risks involved. If you do not understand the correct body positioning when trying to accomplish a yoga pose, you can pull a muscle or otherwise injure yourself. Most gyms and community centers offer beginner yoga classes for a small fee in a friendly environment.

Swimming

Swimming and water aerobatics tend to be called ideal exercises. It is a minimal impact on aerobic fitness exercise that is done in a weightless environment. The health benefit of swimming is that it acts like walking but with the added advantage of having zero effect on your body because of the weightlessness experienced in the water. This makes swimming and water exercise ideal for older adults and folks with injuries or arthritis.

The downside of swimming is the fact that it can require someone to learn how to swim. Water aerobics takes a pool. Many health clubs have indoor, heated pools and provide swimming classes and aerobic water classes.

The equipment necessary for swimming are:

- Swimsuit
- Goggles
- Swim cap

The Dash diet involves an exercise component. Exercise is essential in reducing weight and decreasing blood pressure. The advantages of exercise cannot be emphasized enough.

Select a program or several programs which can be best suited for your way of life and do at least 20 minutes of exercise 3 times a week.

After a month, increase this to 30–45 minutes, up to 5 times a week.

You will not only look better and have lower blood pressure, but you will also FEEL much better as well.

Stress Management

There are undeniable connections among chronic stress, weight gain, and blood pressure. Although we can't always control how stressful our lives are, there are certain steps that each and every one of us can take to better manage the stress we do encounter. Let's take a look at three unique strategies you can employ to help better manage your stress:

Exercise regularly: It should come as no surprise that in a book all about diet and exercise. I'm going to identify exercise as a very important stress-management strategy. Even lower-intensity workouts can make a big difference in overall health. A recent study published in the journal *Health and Place* showed that the simple act of taking a walk outdoors can help lower your stress levels.

Meditate: Meditation is a form of mindfulness that can reap immediate benefits in terms of changing the tide of a stressful day. So many of us are constantly burdened by all of the things going on in our lives, including our own expectations of ourselves and what we face ahead of us in both the short and long term. Secular mindfulness meditation, which can be done in a quiet room in a seated position with your eyes open or closed, is all about breathing naturally while focusing only on the breath and how your body responds to it. You don't want to control your breath, nor do you want your mind to wander. Start with 2 to 3 minutes daily — believe me, it's more challenging than it sounds. Need more support or an extra push? Try a meditation smartphone application such as Calm, Headspace, and The Mindfulness App.

Seek the help of friends and family: Share what's on your mind with someone who you trust but who is not directly related to what is causing you stress. We often underestimate the value of simply getting things off our chests and the effects of simple pleasures like smiling and laughter in helping us mediate the effects of a stressful day.

Sleep

According to the joint consensus statement of both the American Academy of Sleep Medicine and the Sleep Research Society, the recommended level of daily sleep for most adults is at least seven hours but no more than eight. For those who sleep below the recommended minimum of seven hours, there is a growing body of evidence linking insufficient sleep and poor health outcomes. A 2006 study published in the journal *Sleep* found that individuals who slept less than seven hours a night, and especially those who slept under six, had a higher risk of hypertension. Interestingly enough, a 2008 study from the same journal found sleep duration that was either below (5 to 6 hours) or above (9 to 10 hours) recommended levels was associated with weight gain.

If you regularly sleep under 7 hours a night or generally have trouble sleeping well, it may be time to reevaluate your sleep hygiene. For those who may not have heard of this term before, a person's sleep habits are often referred to as their sleep hygiene, and just like good oral hygiene means a good report at your next dentist visit, good sleep hygiene is conducive to a good night's sleep. The CDC recommends focusing on the following things to improve your sleep hygiene:

Consistency: Going to sleep and waking up at similar times all 7 days a week.

Ambiance: Ensuring the bedroom is conducive to sleep by offering a dark, quiet setting at a cool, comfortable temperature. Some of you will prefer slightly warmer or slightly cooler settings, so don't be afraid to experiment to figure out what you feel works best.

Avoid electronics: Make it a hard-and-fast rule to keep your bedroom an electronics-free zone. That includes cell phones! Consider shutting off your devices at least an hour before bedtime and relying on an alarm clock, rather than your phone alarm, to wake you up in the morning. This will make you less reliant on having your phone on or near you while you sleep.

Avoid large amounts of food and drink: Some people may find it easier to sleep if they avoid larger meals or drinking beverages like coffee or alcohol before bedtime. A soothing herbal tea may be an exception to this rule, though.

Physical activity: Being more physically active during the day, rather than later at night, may help you fall asleep more easily.

Chapter 6.

Breakfast Recipes

1 Apple Compote

Preparation time:

15 minutes

Cooking time:

10 minutes

Servings:

4

Ingredients:

- 6 apples, peeled, cored and chopped
- 60ml raw honey
- 1 teaspoon cinnamon powder
- 60ml apple juice
- Sea salt, as much as needed

Directions:

1. Place all ingredients in a saucepan. Stir well, then cook over medium-high heat for 10 minutes or until apples are glazed with honey and lightly salted. Stir constantly. Serve immediately.

Nutrition: Calories: 246 Fats: 0.9g Protein: 1.2g Carbohydrates: 66.3g

Peanut butter and chocolate balls

Preparation time:

45 minutes

Cooking time:

0 minutes

Servings:

15 balls

Ingredients:

- 180ml creamy peanut butter
- 60g of unsweetened cocoa powder
- 2 tablespoons softened almond butter
- 1/2 teaspoon of vanilla extract
- 250g maple sugar

Directions:

1. Line a baking sheet with parchment paper. Combine all ingredients in a bowl. Mix well.
2. Divide the mixture into 15 parts and shape each part into a 2cm ball. Place the balls on the baking sheet and refrigerate for at least 30 minutes, then serve cold.

Nutrition: Calories: 146 Fats: 8.1g Protein: 4.2g Carbohydrates: 16.9g

3 Sweet and spicy pecans

Preparation time:

15 minutes

Cooking time:

17 minutes

Servings:

4

Ingredients:

- 250g pecans, cut in half
- 3 tablespoons almond butter
- 1 teaspoon cinnamon powder
- 1/2 teaspoon ground nutmeg
- 60ml raw honey
- 1/4 teaspoon sea salt

Directions:

1. Preheat oven to 180°C. Line a baking sheet with parchment paper. Combine all ingredients in a bowl. Mix well, then spread the mixture into the single layer on the baking sheet with a spatula.
2. Bake in the preheated oven for 16 minutes or until the pecan halves are nicely browned. Serve immediately.

Nutrition: Calories: 324 Fats: 29.8g Protein: 3.2g Carbohydrates: 13.9g

Lemon Cake 4

Preparation time:

15 minutes

Cooking time:

1 hour and 30 minutes

Servings:

8

Ingredients:

- 65g coconut flour
- 160g of almond flour
- 3 tbsp. Stevia sweetener
- 2 teaspoons. Baking powder
- 1/2 teaspoon. Xanthan gum
- 120ml fresh cream
- 113g butter, melted
- 1 tablespoon. Freshly squeezed fruit juices
- Peel of a large lemon
- 2 eggs

Directions:

1. Grease a baking sheet with butter or cooking spray. Mix together coconut flour, almond flour, stevia, baking powder and xanthan gum in a bowl. In another bowl, combine the fresh cream, butter, lemon juice, lemon zest and eggs. Mix until well combined.
2. Gradually pour the wet ingredients over the dry ingredients and mix to create a smooth batter. Spread the batter in the baking dish and bake at 160°C for 1 hour and 30 minutes.

Nutrition: Calories: 350 Carbohydrates: 11.1g Protein: 17.6g Fats: 32.6g

Preparation time:

15 minutes

Cooking time:

30 minutes

Servings:

12

Ingredients:

- 60g raw oat flour
- 1/2 teaspoon baking powder
- 1/2 teaspoon of iodized salt
- 60g dry milk
- 60ml vegetable oil
- 1/4 teaspoon baking soda
- 70g of sugar
- 165g of flour
- 230ml of milk
- 120g of blueberries

Directions:

1. Preheat oven to 175°C. Coat muffin cups with vegetable oil.
2. Mix flour, baking soda, baking powder, oats, sugar and salt in a bowl. Mix milk, dry milk, eggs and vegetable oil in another bowl.
3. Add blueberries and stir until the consistency becomes lumpy. Pour into muffin cups.
4. Bake for 30 minutes until muffins turn golden brown on the edges.
5. Serve immediately warm or place in an airtight container and store in the refrigerator to cool.

Nutrition: Calories 150 Sodium 180 mg Carbohydrates 22 g Protein 4 g Fat 5 g Fiber 1 g

Preparation time:

10 minutes

Cooking time:

5 minutes

Servings:

2

Ingredients:

- 4 eggs
- A pinch of black pepper
- 2 tablespoons chopped cooked ham
- 40g low-fat cheddar, shredded
- 2 tablespoons chopped parsley
- Cooking spray

Directions:

1. Inside a bowl, combine eggs with pepper, ham, cheese and parsley and whisk effectively.
2. Grease a skillet with cooking spray, add the egg mixture, cook for 4-5 minutes.
3. Divide waffles among plates and serve for breakfast.
4. Enjoy.

Nutrition: Calories: 200 Total Fats: 7g Total carbohydrates: 29g Fiber: 3g Sugar: 0g Protein: 3g

7 | Breakfast Fruit Bowl

Preparation time:

5 minutes

Cooking time:

5 minutes

Servings:

2

Ingredients:

- 125g mango, chopped
- 1 banana, sliced
- 130g pineapple, chopped
- 230ml almond milk

Directions:

1. Prepare a bowl, combine the mango, banana, pineapple and almond milk.
2. Stir, divide into smaller bowls and serve for breakfast

Nutrition: Calories: 103 Total Fats: 0g Total carbohydrates: 25g Fiber: 0g Sugar: 0g Protein: 1g

Egg whites breakfast mix 8

Preparation time:

10 minutes

Cooking time:

10 minutes

Servings:

4

Ingredients:

- 1 yellow onion, chopped
- 3 plum tomatoes, chopped
- 300g. spinach, chopped
- Pinch of black pepper
- 2 tablespoons water
- 12 egg whites
- Cooking spray

Directions:

1. Mix egg whites with water and pepper in a bowl. Grease a skillet with cooking spray, heat over medium heat, add 1/4 of the egg whites, spread in the skillet and cook for 2 minutes.
2. Add the spinach, tomatoes and onion, fold and add to a plate. Serve for breakfast.

Nutrition: Calories: 31 kcal Carbohydrates: 0 g Fats: 2 g Protein: 3 g Sodium: 55 mg

Green berry and beet smoothie

9

Preparation time:

10 minutes

Cooking time:

0 minutes

Servings:

2

Ingredients:

- 200ml unsweetened almond milk
- 95g of chopped beets
- 1 small beet, peeled, chopped
- Juice of 1/2 orange
- 90g frozen mixed berries
- 1/2 medium banana, sliced, frozen

Directions:

1. Pour orange juice and almond milk into blender. Put in the beet greens, beet, berries and banana.
2. Blend until smooth pureed.
3. Pour into 2 glasses and serve with ice if desired.

Nutrition: Calories: 84 Fats: 1.5 g Total Carbohydrates: 18 g Protein: 2 g Sodium: 127 mg

Strawberry smoothie [10]

Preparation time:

5 minutes

Cooking time:

0 minutes

Servings:

2

Ingredients:

- 250g low-salt, low-fat ricotta cheese
- 200g fresh or frozen strawberries
- 320ml of milk

Directions:

1. Combine the ricotta, strawberries and milk in a blender. Blend until a smooth puree is obtained.
2. Pour into 2 glasses and serve with ice if desired.

Nutrition: Calories: 215 Fats: 2.8 g Total Carbohydrates: 26 g Protein: 22 g Sodium: 122 mg

Chapter 7

Fish and Seafood Recipes

11 Air Fried Branzino

Preparation Time:

10 minutes

Cooking Time:

10 minutes

Servings:

2

Ingredients:

- 1 lemon zest, grated
- 1 orange zest, grated
- ½ lemon, juiced
- ½ orange, juiced
- Salt and black pepper, to taste
- 4 medium branzino fillets, boneless
- ½ cup parsley, chopped
- 2 Tbsp olive oil
- A pinch red pepper flakes, crushed

Directions:

1. Mix the fish fillets with lemon zest, orange zest, lemon juice, orange juice, salt, pepper, oil and pepper flakes in a clean and large bowl.
2. Toss perfectly and move the fillets to an Air Fryer, preheated at 350°F
3. Bake for 10 minutes, flipping the fillets once.
4. Divide fish into different plates, sprinkle with parsley and serve immediately.
5. Enjoy!

Nutrition: Calories: 228 kcal Total Fat: 17 g Total Carbohydrates: 0 g Fiber: 0 g Sugar: 0 g Protein: 17 g

Cod with Pearl Onions 12

Preparation Time:
10 minutes

Cooking Time:
15 minutes

Servings:
2

Ingredients:
- 14 oz. pearl onions
- 2 medium cod fillets
- 1 Tbsp parsley, dried
- 1 tsp thyme
- Black dried pepper, to taste
- 8 oz. mushrooms, sliced

Directions:
1. Put the fish in a heat-proof dish that fits your Air Fryer. Add onions, parsley, mushrooms, thyme and black pepper.
2. Toss well to coat, place in your air fryer, cook at 350°F for 15 minutes.
3. Divide all of it into different plates and serve immediately.
4. Enjoy.

Nutrition: Calories: 178 kcal Total Fat: 1.8 g Total Carbohydrates: 15.8 g Fiber: 1.5 g Sugar: 0 g Protein: 22.9 g

13 Chipotle Spiced Shrimp

Preparation Time:

5 minutes

Cooking Time:

5 minutes

Servings:

2

Ingredients

- ¾ lb. uncooked shrimp
- 2 Tbsp tomato paste
- 1 ½ tsp water
- ½ tsp olive oil
- ½ tsp minced garlic
- ½ tsp chipotle chili powder
- ½ tsp fresh oregano
- 1 tsp lemon juice
- ½ minced green chili

Directions:

1. Clean the shrimp in cold water and pat dry with a paper towel.
2. Combine oil, water and tomato paste in a bowl.
3. Add oregano, chili powder, minced green chili, lemon juice and garlic to the tomato paste mixture. Mix well.
4. Brush the shrimps with the marinade. Place the shrimps in the refrigerator.
5. Heat a gas grill. Coat the gas grill with cooking spray. Position the cooking rack 4 to 6 inches from the heat source.
6. Put the shrimp on skewers and put it on the grill. Turn the shrimps after 3 to 4 minutes. Transfer the shrimps to a plate once they are cooked.

Nutrition: Calories: 152 kcal Total Fat: 3 g Total Carbohydrates: 5 g Fiber: 0.3 g Sugar: 2 g Protein: 24 g

Preparation Time:

10 minutes

Cooking Time:

14 minutes

Servings:

2

Ingredients:

- 1 tsp lemon zest, grated
- 4 white bread slices, quartered
- ¼ cup walnuts, chopped
- ¼ cup parmesan, grated
- 4 Tbsp olive oil
- 4 sole fillets, boneless
- Salt and black pepper, to taste
- 4 Tbsp butter
- ¼ cup lemon juice
- 3 Tbsp capers
- 2 garlic cloves, minced
- 2 bunches Swiss chard, chopped

Directions:

1. Mix the bread with walnuts, cheese and lemon zest in a food processor; pulse well.
2. Add about half of the olive oil. Pulse well again.
3. Keep it aside for a while.
4. Heat the pan with the butter over medium heat, and add lemon juice, salt, pepper and capers.
5. Stir gently and add fish. Toss it. Move the fish to your preheated Air Fryer's basket.
6. Top with some bread mix you already made at the start.
7. Cook at 350°F for 14 minutes.
8. Also, heat another pan containing the remaining oil, then add garlic, Swiss chard, salt and pepper.
9. Stir the resulting mixture gently, cook for about 2 minutes, and remove the heat.
10. Divide the fish into different plates
11. Serve with sautéed chard on the side.
12. Enjoy!

Nutrition: Calories: 160 kcal Total Fat: 3 g Total Carbohydrates: 4 g Fiber: 1 g Sugar: 1 g Protein: 29 g

Hawaiian Salmon

Preparation Time:

10 minutes

Cooking Time:

10 minutes

Servings:

2

Ingredients:

- 20 oz. canned pineapple pieces and juice
- ½ tsp ginger, grated
- 2 tsp garlic powder
- 1 tsp onion powder
- 1 Tbsp balsamic vinegar
- 2 medium salmon fillets, boneless
- Salt and black pepper, to taste

Directions:

1. Season the salmon with garlic powder, onion powder, salt and black pepper. Rub well.
2. Move to a heat-proof dish that fits into your air fryer.
3. Add the ginger and pineapple chunk. Toss them gently.
4. Drizzle the vinegar all over, place gently in your air fryer, and cook at 350°F for 10 minutes.
5. Divide all of it into different plates and serve.
6. Enjoy!

Nutrition: Calories: 261 kcal Total Fat: 12 g Total Carbohydrates: 8 g Fiber: 1.3 g Sugar: 4 g Protein: 29 g

Marinated Salmon

Preparation Time:

30 minutes

Cooking Time:

20 minutes

Servings:

2

Ingredients:

- 1 whole salmon
- 1 Tbsp dill, chopped
- 1 Tbsp tarragon, chopped
- 1 Tbsp garlic, minced
- 2 lemons, juiced
- 1 lemon, sliced
- A pinch salt and black pepper

Directions:

1. Mix with salt, pepper and lemon juice, and cover the large fish.
2. Toss well to coat and keep in the fridge for about an hour.
3. Stuff the salmon with garlic and lemon slices.
4. Then, introduce it to your Air Fryer's basket and cook at 320°F for 25 minutes.
5. Divide into different plates
6. Finally, serve with a tasty coleslaw on the side.
7. Enjoy!

Nutrition: Calories: 310 kcal Total Fat: 21 g Total Carbohydrates: 1 g Fiber: 0 g Sugar: 0 g Protein: 29 g

Preparation Time:

10 minutes

Cooking Time:

14 minutes

Servings:

2

Ingredients:

- 2 red snapper fillets, boneless
- 1 Tbsp olive oil
- ½ cup red bell pepper, chopped
- ½ cup green bell pepper, chopped
- ½ cup leeks, chopped
- Salt and black pepper, to taste
- 1 tsp tarragon, dried
- A splash white wine

Directions:

1. In a heat-proof dish that fits your Air Fryer, mix fish fillets with salt, pepper, oil, green bell pepper, red bell pepper, leeks, tarragon and wine.
2. Toss everything properly to coat.
3. Then, introduce it into a preheated air fryer at 350°F. Cook for about 14 minutes.
4. Flip the fish fillets halfway.
5. Divide the fish and veggies into different plates and serve while still warm.
6. Enjoy!

Nutrition: Calories: 340 kcal Total Fat: 11 g Total Carbohydrates: 26 g Fiber: 3 g Sugar: 3 g Protein: 37 g

18 | Scallop and Veg Skewers

Preparation Time:

10 minutes

Cooking Time:

25 minutes

Servings:

2

Ingredients:

- 1 lb. scallops
- 1 Tbsp olive oil
- ½ lemon, juiced
- ½ tsp thyme
- 2 shallots, peeled and halved
- 2 bell peppers, cut into thick chunks
- 6 cherry tomatoes
- ½ zucchini, cut into chunks
- Ground black pepper, to taste
- Skewers, soaked in water

Directions:

1. In a bowl, combine the oil, lemon juice, thyme and pepper. Mix well before adding the scallops and covering. Leave the scallops in the marinade for 20 minutes.
2. While the scallops marinade, preheat your broiler/grill.
3. Skewer the vegetables and scallops in an alternating fashion.
4. Season with pepper.
5. Place under the heat source and cook for about 3 minutes per side.

Nutrition: Calories: 400 kcal Total Fat: 25 g Total Carbohydrates: 18 g Fiber: 2 g Sugar: 5 g Protein: 30 g

Chapter 8

Meat Recipes
(Beef, Pork, and Lamb)

Special Sausage

Preparation Time:

10 minutes

Cooking Time:

10 minutes

Servings:

2

Ingredients:

- 1 pound sausages, sliced
- 1 red bell pepper, cut into strips
- ½ cup yellow onion, chopped.
- ½ cup chicken stock
- 1/3 cup ketchup
- 3 Tbsp brown sugar
- 2 Tbsp mustard
- 2 Tbsp apple cider vinegar

Directions:

1. Mix the sugar with ketchup, mustard, stock and cider vinegar in a clean bowl. Whisk well.
2. Mix the sausage slices with bell pepper, onion and sweet-and-sour mix in your fryer's pan.
3. Then, toss and cook at 350°F for 10 minutes.
4. Divide into different bowls and serve.

Nutrition: Calories: 191 kcal Total Fat: 10 g Total Carbohydrates: 14 g Fiber: 4 g Sugar: 7 g Protein: 13 g

Beef Stroganoff 20

Preparation Time:
10 minutes

Cooking Time:
15 minutes

Servings:
2

Ingredients

- ½ cup onion
- ½ lb. boneless beef (fat removed)
- 4 cups yolkless egg noodles
- ½ can fat-free mushroom cream
- 1 Tbsp all-purpose flour
- ½ tsp. paprika
- 1/8 tsp black pepper
- 1/8 tsp white pepper
- ½ cup fat-free sour cream

Directions:

1. Sauté the onions in a non-stick pan till the onions become translucent.
2. Add the beef into the pan and continue cooking till the beef turns brown and tender.
3. Take off the beef from the heat once cooked.
4. Fill a large pot with water and bring the water to a boil.
5. Place the noodles into the pot and cook as per the packet directions.
6. Drain with cold water once the noodles are cooked.
7. Add the soup mixture to the non-stick pan. Add the salt, black pepper, white pepper and paprika to the soup mixture.
8. Add the beef into this mixture as well, and once the mixture is warmed, remove it from the heat. Add the sour cream after removing it from the heat.

Nutrition: Calories: 391 kcal Total Fat: 23 g Total Carbohydrates: 21 g Fiber: 1.3 g Sugar: 2 g Protein: 25 g

Pork Chops with Tomato Curry

Preparation Time:

15 minutes

Cooking Time:

25 minutes

Servings:

2

Ingredients:

- 6 pork loin chops, boneless (6 oz. each)
- 1 small onion
- 4 tsp butter (divided)
- 3 medium apples, sliced thinly
- 1 can whole tomatoes, undrained
- 4 tsp sugar
- 2 tsp curry powder
- ½ tsp salt
- ½ tsp chili powder
- 4 cups hot cooked brown rice
- 2 Tbsp toasted slivered almonds, optional

Directions:

1. Finely chopped the onion.
2. Prepare a stockpot, warm 2 tsp butter over medium-high heat. Brown pork chops in batches. Remove from the pan.
3. Warm the remaining butter in the same pan over medium heat. Include onions; keep cooking and stirring for 2–3 minutes or until softened.
4. Keep turning the apples, tomatoes, sugar, curry powder, salt and chili powder. Gather to a boil, stirring consciously to break up tomatoes.
5. Return the chops to the pan. Reduce heat; simmer, uncovered, for 5 minutes. Keep turning the chops; cook it up to 3–5 minutes longer or until a thermometer inserted in the pork reads 145°.
6. Allow it to cool for 5 minutes minimum, before serving. Serve with rice and, if desired, sprinkle with almonds.

Nutrition: Calories: 143 kcal Total Fat: 6 g Total Carbohydrates: 9 g Fiber: 2 g Sugar: 6 g Protein: 12 g

Preparation Time:

10 minutes

Cooking Time:

30 minutes

Servings:

2

Ingredients:

- 12 oz. pork tenderloin
- 1 potato, large, cut into ½" cubes
- ¾ cups apple cider
- ¼ cup apple cider vinegar
- ¼ tsp paprika, smoked
- 2 Tbsp maple syrup
- ¼ tsp ginger, dried
- 1 tsp ginger, fresh, minced
- 2 Tbsp vegetable oil
- 1 apple, cut into ½" cube size

Directions:

1. Take a large bowl and start mixing smoked paprika, apple cider, maple syrup, apple cider vinegar, black pepper and ginger, and keep aside.
2. Set your oven at 360°F and preheat.
3. Take a large oven-safe sauté pan and heat oil at medium temperature.
4. Once the oil becomes hot, put the pork tenderloin. Continue cooking at medium temperature for about 10 minutes.
5. Flip sides and make sure to cook all sides evenly. Once the sides are cooked well, remove them from the heat.
6. Arrange the sweet potatoes around the tenderloin. Pour the apple cider mixture over it.
7. Cover the saucepan and bake it for about 10 minutes.
8. Place the sliced apple pieces around the pork tenderloin and bake for another 10 minutes until the tenderloin temperature shows 340°F.
9. Once the temperature is reached 340°F, stop baking and remove the pork tenderloin, potatoes, and apple, and allow it to settle for 10 minutes.
10. Heat the cider mixture and reduce to ¼ cup.
11. Slice the pork into edible sizes. Serve along with sweet potatoes and apples.
12. Dress it with apple cider while serving.

Nutrition: Calories: 339 kcal Total Fat: 12 g Total Carbohydrates: 21 g Fiber: 3 g Sugar: 0 g Protein: 35 g

23 Savory Pork Loin

Preparation Time:

5 minutes

Cooking Time:

30 minutes

Servings:

2

Ingredients:

- Non-stick cooking spray (optional)
- 2 lbs. boneless pork loin
- 1 ½ Tbsp chopped fresh rosemary
- 1 ½ Tbsp fresh thyme, chopped
- 2 garlic cloves, minced
- ¼ tsp ground black pepper

Directions:

1. Preheat the oven to 350°F.
2. Prepare a roasting pan with aluminum foil or with non-stick cooking spray.
3. In a small bowl, mix the rosemary, thyme, garlic and pepper. Season the pork loin with this rub.
4. Transfer to the prepared roasting pan and bake for 25 to 30 minutes, or the pork loin's internal temperature has reached 145°F.
5. Let it rest for a couple of minutes before slicing. Portion the pork into 6 storage containers.

Nutrition: Calories: 227 kcal Total Fat: 9 g Total Carbohydrates: 8 g Fiber: 1 g Sugar: 2 g Protein: 28 g

Preparation Time:

5 minutes

Cooking Time:

20 minutes

Servings:

2

Ingredients:

- 2 ½ Tbsp honey
- 4 garlic cloves, minced
- 1 Tbsp reduced-sodium soy sauce
- 1 Tbsp no-salt-added ketchup
- ½ tsp freshly ground black pepper
- ½ tsp dried oregano
- 4 (6 oz.) bone-in loin pork chops, fat trimmed
- 1 Tbsp extra-virgin olive oil
- 1 Tbsp unsalted butter

Directions:

1. Preheat the oven to 400°F.
2. Mix honey, garlic, soy sauce, ketchup, pepper and oregano in a mixing bowl.
3. Add pork chops to a bowl and pour the sauce over them. Mix until fully coated.
4. Prepare a large oven-safe skillet, heat the oil over medium-high heat.
5. Add the chops with sauce to the skillet. Cook for 2 minutes per side, until brown slightly. Remove from the heat.
6. Add ¾ tsp of butter to the top of each pork chop. Transfer to the oven and bake for 15 to 18 minutes, or until the pork reaches an internal temperature of 145°F.
7. Let it cool, then place a chop in each of the 4 storage Containers. Divide the pan sauce evenly over the portions.

Nutrition: Calories: 204 kcal Total Fat: 6 g Total Carbohydrates: 18 g Fiber: 0.2 g Sugar: 16 g Protein: 20 g

Chapter 9.
Poultry Recipes

Preparation Time:

5 minutes

Cooking Time:

15–20 minutes

Servings:

2

Ingredients:

- 4 lb. chicken breast, skinless and boneless
- 1 tsp mixture blackening spice
- 1 cup Romaine lettuce
- 2 Radishes
- 2 Pepper strips
- 3 Grated carrots
- 1 Tomato
- 1 Red cabbage
- 1 cup Peas
- 1 cup Peapods

For garnishing:
- Blueberries
- Raspberries
- Sliced strawberries

Directions:

1. Marinate the meat with the mixture of blackening spice and grill at 165°F.
2. Use the strips of lettuce to make the salad base.
3. Add radishes, pepper strips, grated carrots, tomato, red cabbage and peas, as well as pea pods.
4. Top with your favorite berry mixture: blueberries, raspberries and sliced strawberries.
5. Slice the chicken breast into long thin strips and serve them on the salad top.
6. Add your favorite dressing with low sodium content.

Nutrition: Calories: 251 kcal Total Fat: 14 g Total Carbohydrates: 8 g Fiber: 2 g Sugar: 1.7 g Protein: 18 g

26 Curried Chicken wrap

Preparation Time:

10 minutes

Cooking Time:

10 minutes

Servings:

2

Ingredients:

- 2 medium whole-wheat tortillas
- 1/3 cup cooked chicken, chopped
- 1 cup apple, chopped
- 1 Tbsp light mayonnaise
- 1 tsp curry powder
- 1 cup, or about 15, raw baby carrots

Directions:

1. Mix all the ingredients, except for the tortillas.
2. Divide and place at the center of the tortillas.
3. Roll and serve.

Nutrition: Calories: 380 kcal Total Fat: 9 g Total Carbohydrates: 47 g Fiber: 4 g Sugar: 5 g Protein: 27 g

French Country Chicken

Preparation Time:

10 minutes

Cooking Time:

15 minutes

Servings:

2

Ingredients

- 4 boneless chicken breasts
- 1 Tbsp olive oil
- 4 sliced shallots
- ¼ pound sliced mushrooms
- 1 Tbsp plain flour
- 1 cup low sodium chicken stock
- 1 Tbsp fresh rosemary
- 2 Tbsp chopped parsley
- ¼ tsp black pepper
- ¼ tsp white pepper
- Salt, to taste

Directions:

1. Place the chicken breasts between wax paper. Flatten the chicken breasts using a mallet.
2. Cut each chicken breast in half. Cover the chicken breasts with plastic wrap and refrigerate the breasts till they become firm.
3. Warm the olive oil in a pan over medium heat. Sauté the shallots in the olive oil for about 3 minutes. Add the mushrooms to the pan and sauté them for about 2 minutes.
4. Combine ¼ cup low sodium chicken stock and flour in a bowl.
5. Add the flour mixture to the pan. Stir in the remaining chicken stock in the pan and cook the mixture over medium heat.
6. Put salt, black pepper and white pepper into the sauce. Let the sauce thicken and allow it to cook for 5 minutes. Get the pan from the heat and put the rosemary.
7. Add about a Tbsp of olive oil to a non-stick skillet. Add the chicken breasts till they are no longer pink.
8. When serving the chicken breasts, transfer them to a platter and add some mushroom sauce over the chicken breasts. Garnish with chopped parsley.

Nutrition: Calories: 210 kcal Total Fat: 8 g Total Carbohydrates: 5 g Fiber: 0 g Sugar: 0 g Protein: 27 g

Preparation Time:

20 minutes

Cooking Time:

20 minutes

Servings:

2

Ingredients:

For Cauliflower Rice
- 1 small cauliflower head
- 2 Tbsp chicken bone bread
- ¼ tsp sea salt
- 1 Tbsp coconut oil

For Sesame Ginger Chicken Stir
- 1 ½ cups original chicken bone bread
- 2 Tbsp tapioca starch
- 1 lb. boneless chicken breasts, chopped
- 1 medium red bell pepper, chopped
- ¼ tsp organic crushed red pepper
- 1 Tbsp coconut oil
- 3 garlic cloves, minced
- 1 Tbsp grated fresh ginger
- ½ tsp sea salt
- 1 lb. asparagus, chopped
- 4 oz. Shiitake mushrooms, chopped
- 2 Tbsp organic toasted sesame seeds

Directions:

1. Using a food processor, pulse the cauliflower head in batches until the texture is good enough for cauliflower rice.
2. Put the coconut oil in a skillet on medium-high heat and add the cauliflower; cook for 2 minutes and stir.
3. Stir in the bone broth and sea salt. Cook for the next 5 minutes until soft. Set aside.
4. Mix tapioca, bone broth and crushed red pepper till they are smooth; set it aside. Place a large skillet on medium-high heat and add coconut oil.
5. Put the chicken and fry for 5 minutes to become crispy. Take off the skillet. Stir into the skillet onions, ginger, garlic and salt, and cook for 3 minutes.
6. Stir in the mixture of bone broth and stir continuously for 2 minutes over medium heat until thickened. Add the chicken; stir fry to mix well. Sprinkle them with sesame seeds.
7. Serve it with cauliflower rice.

Nutrition: Calories: 225 kcal Total Fat: 5 g Total Carbohydrates: 23 g Fiber: 1 g Sugar: 10 g Protein: 25 g

Chapter 10.

Soup Recipes

Creamy Butternut Squash Soup

Preparation Time:

10 minutes

Cooking Time:

30 minutes

Servings:

2

Ingredients:

- 2 ¼ lbs. butternut squash
- 1 cup chopped onion
- 1 Tbsp grated fresh ginger
- 1 Tbsp unsalted butter
- 3 cups low sodium vegetable broth (or chicken broth)

Directions:

1. Preheat oven to 450°F.
2. Slice the squash in half lengthwise, take out the seeds, and place cut side down on a baking sheet.
3. Roast the squash until it's tender. Wait for it to cool.
4. While the squash is roasting, sauté the ginger and onion in the butter until soft.
5. Put the broth, then cover and let it cook for 10 minutes.
6. Prepare the squash by taking off the skin.
7. Put half squash and half of the broth in a blender; mix until smooth.
8. Repeat with the remaining ingredients. If needed, put some water to achieve the desired consistency.
9. Return the soup to the saucepan and reheat.
10. Salt and pepper, to taste.

Nutrition: Calories: 160 kcal Total Fat: 11 g Total Carbohydrates: 0 g Fiber: 0 g Sugar: 8 g Protein: 0 g

Preparation Time:

10 minutes

Cooking Time:

20 minutes

Servings:

2

Ingredients:

- 2 Tbsp olive oil
- 1 Tbsp balsamic vinegar
- 1 yellow or white onion, chopped
- 3 garlic cloves, minced
- 2 lbs. tomatoes, deseeded, chopped
- ¼ tsp red pepper flakes
- 1 Tbsp brown sugar
- ½ tsp dried thyme
- 4 small slices white bread, crust removed
- 1 ½ cup vegetable stock or low-sodium chicken
- Black pepper

Directions:

1. Add and warm oil in a large saucepan or stockpot.
2. Add the onions and garlic; sauté for 5 minutes.
3. Put tomatoes, then pepper, sugar, thyme and bread. Let it cook for 3 minutes.
4. Transfer to a food processor or blender. Mix well.
5. Carefully put the stock and let it boil for 10 minutes.
6. Put vinegar and cook another two minutes.

Nutrition: Calories: 52 kcal Total Fat: 0 g Total Carbohydrates: 9 g Fiber: 0 g Sugar: 9 g Protein: 0 g

Savory Tomato Lentil Soup

Preparation Time:

10 minutes

Cooking Time:

30 minutes

Servings:

2

Ingredients:

- Garlic, as much as desired, minced
- 1 medium onion, diced
- 3 medium carrots, diced
- 2 Tbsp olive oil
- 2 stalks celery, chopped
- 6 cups vegetable stock
- 1 can (28 oz.) diced tomatoes, including juice or 5–8 diced fresh tomatoes with ¼ cup water
- 2 cups cooked or canned lentils
- Pepper, to taste
- Cayenne pepper, to taste
- 1 cup dry pasta

Directions:

1. Sauté garlic, onions and carrots until translucent.
2. Add the celery, stock, tomatoes, lentils, pepper and cayenne, and bring to a boil.
3. Reduce the heat to low and simmer for 20 minutes or until carrots are tender.
4. Add pasta and simmer for 10 more minutes before serving.

Nutrition: Calories: 140 kcal Total Fat: 0 g Total Carbohydrates: 27 g Fiber: 6 g Sugar: 5 g Protein: 8 g

Avocado Cucumber Soup 32

Preparation Time:

10 minutes

Cooking Time:

20–30 minutes

Servings:

2

Ingredients:

- ½ cucumber
- 1 small spring onion
- 1 avocado pulp
- ½ lemon, juiced
- 1 Tbsp chives (chopped up)
- Fresh black pepper
- 1 low-fat yogurt
- 1 slice wholegrain bread

Directions:

1. Prepare the cucumber by peeling and cutting it into pieces.
2. Remove the pulp from the avocado.
3. Wash and chop the spring onions.
4. Put everything together with the yogurt and the juice of the ½ lime in a blender, and puree.
5. Then, place in a soup plate, garnish with the chives and pour some fresh black pepper over it.
6. Enjoy with the slice of whole-meal bread.

Nutrition: Calories: 169 kcal Total Fat: 8 g Total Carbohydrates: 15 g Fiber: 3 g Sugar: 8 g Protein: 12 g

Chapter 11.

Vegetable Recipes

33 | Bell Pepper Mackerel

Preparation Time:

10 minutes

Cooking Time:

15–20 minutes

Servings:

2

Ingredients:

- 450 g mackerel (preferably fresh; otherwise 100 g mackerel fillets)
- 2 pointed peppers (alternatively: ½ yellow, ½ red peppers)
- 1 tomato
- 1 small onion
- Coconut fat
- 1 tsp thyme leaves
- 1 Tbsp wild garlic (cut)
- 4 black olives
- Black pepper (fresh)
- 4 slices whole-grain baguette

Directions:

1. Clean, core, and cut the bell pepper into strips.
2. Wash the tomato and cut it into slices.
3. Peel the onion and cut it into rings.
4. Prepare the herbs.
5. Sauté the onions in a pan with a little coconut fat until they are translucent.
6. Wash the mackerel, dry it, put it in the pan, and fry it briefly.
7. Then add the bell pepper and tomato slices, and pour the herbs on top.
8. Put a lid on the pan and cook for about 10–12 minutes.
9. Cut the olives into slices and lightly toast the whole-grain baguette.
10. Arrange the fish on a plate. Garnish with olive slices and sprinkle with a little black pepper.

Nutrition: Calories: 270 kcal Total Fat: 21 g Total Carbohydrates: 4 g Fiber: 2 g Sugar: 0 g Protein: 22 g

Preparation Time:

5 minutes

Cooking Time:

10 minutes

Servings:

2

Ingredients:

- 1 fresh pineapple
- 2 Tbsp brown sugar
- 2 Tbsp lime juice
- 1 Tbsp olive oil
- 1 Tbsp honey or agave nectar
- 1 ½ tsp chili powder
- Dash salt

Directions:

1. Peel the pineapple, removing any eyes from the fruit.
2. Cut lengthwise into wedges; take away the core. In a very little bowl, combine the remaining ingredients till blended.
3. Brush the pineapple with half the glaze; reserve the remaining mixture for basting.
4. Grill the pineapple for 2–4 minutes on each side or until lightly browned, occasionally basting with the reserved glaze.

Nutrition: Calories: 97 kcal Total Fat: 2 g Total Carbohydrates: 20 g Fiber: 1 g Sugar: 17 g Protein: 1 g

Spinach Salad with Walnuts and Strawberry

35

Preparation Time:

10 minutes

Cooking Time:

15 minutes

Servings:

2

Ingredients:

- ½ cup walnuts
- 4 cups fresh spinach, loosely trimmed stems
- 3 Tbsp honey
- 2 Tbsp spicy brown mustard
- ¼ cup balsamic vinegar
- ¼ tsp sea salt
- ¼ cup crumbled Feta cheese (about 1 oz.), optional

Directions:

1. Heat the oven until 375°F.
2. Arrange the walnuts on a rimmed baking sheet and bake for 8 minutes until they are fragrant and toasted. Switch to a cool plate.
3. Place the spinach in a large container. The honey, mustard, vinegar and salt are whisked together in a small cup.
4. Drizzle the salad with over ¾ of the dressing and scatter the walnuts on top.
5. Serve sprinkled with both the cheese (if it is used) and the remaining side dressing.

Nutrition: Calories: 129 kcal Total Fat: 8 g Total Carbohydrates: 10 g Fiber: 3 g Sugar: 0.8 g Protein: 6.6 g

Veggie Sushi

Preparation Time:

10 minutes

Cooking Time:

15 minutes

Servings:

2

Ingredients:

- 3 cups brown rice
- 2 Tbsp rice wine vinegar
- 2 avocados, longitudinally cut
- 2 carrots, longitudinally sliced
- 1 Cucumber, longitudinally sliced
- Ponzu sauce, to taste

Directions:

1. Cook the brown rice, as indicated in the instructions. Fold the rice into the vinegar rice wine. Let the cooked rice cool down.
2. When cool, spread the rice uniformly with a wooden spoon on a bamboo sushi mat, or dip your hands in a cold bowl of water and spread the rice with your fingertips; on top, layer avocado, cabbage and slices of cucumber.
3. Using the mat to roll it into a packed roll of rice and vegetable, slide the mat out and repeat.
4. Slice into circles of ½ inch. Serve.

Nutrition: Calories: 135 kcal Total Fat: 3 g Total Carbohydrates: 22 g Fiber: 2 g Sugar: 5 g Protein: 3 g

Chapter 12.

Fruit Recipes

37 Fruit and Nut Bar

Preparation Time:

10 minutes

Cooking Time:

20 minutes

Servings:

2

Ingredients:

- ½ cup quinoa flour
- ½ cup oats
- ¼ cup flaxseed flour
- ¼ cup wheat germ
- ¼ cup chopped almonds
- ¼ cup chopped dried apricots
- ¼ cup chopped dried figs
- ¼ cup honey
- ¼ cup chopped dried pineapple
- 2 Tbsp cornstarch

Directions:

1. Heat the oven at 300°F.
2. Place parchment on a sheet pan.
3. Mix all the ingredients thoroughly.
4. Pour the mixture into the pan.
5. Bake for 20 minutes.
6. Cool completely before cutting into pieces.

Nutrition: Calories: 109 kcal Total Fat: 2 g Total Carbohydrates: 20 g Fiber: 0 g Sugar: 8 g Protein: 1 g

Fruit Salad

Preparation Time:
10 minutes

Cooking Time:
5 minutes

Servings:
2

Ingredients:
- 1 tsp vanilla extract
- 1 watermelon, peeled and chopped
- 1 cup strawberries, chopped
- 1 cup kiwis, peeled and chopped
- 1 cup blueberries
- 1 tsp coconut sugar
- 8 oz. non-fat yogurt
- 8 oz. low-fat cream cheese

Directions:
1. In a bowl, combine the watermelon with vanilla, strawberries, kiwis, blueberries, sugar, yogurt and cream cheese; toss.
2. Divide into small cups and serve cold.
3. Enjoy!

Nutrition: Calories: 110 kcal Total Fat: 0 g Total Carbohydrates: 17 g Fiber: 0 g Sugar: 0 g Protein: 2 g

Fruit Skewers with Vanilla Honey Yogurt Dip

Preparation Time:

10 minutes

Cooking Time:

10 minutes

Servings:

2

Ingredients:

Fruit Skewers:

- 10 strawberries
- 20 blueberries
- 1 pineapple, cored and cubed
- 2 kiwis, peeled and cubed
- 10 bamboo skewers

Vanilla Yogurt Dip:

- ½ cup non-fat Greek yogurt
- 8 oz. non-fat or low-fat cream cheese
- ¼ cup honey
- 1 tsp vanilla extract

Directions:

1. Cut up the pineapple and kiwis into even squares.
2. Take the blueberries, strawberries, kiwis and pineapple squares, and place them onto the skewers in a rainbow color order.
3. Then create the yogurt dip; combine yogurt, cream cheese, honey and vanilla extract in a bowl. Mix well until combined.
4. Plate the fruits on a serving dish and serve with the vanilla yogurt dip.

Nutrition: Calories: 215 kcal Total Fat: 3 g Total Carbohydrates: 50 g Fiber: 5 g Sugar: 30 g Protein: 4 g

Preparation Time:

5 minutes

Cooking Time:

5 minutes

Servings:

2

Ingredients:

- 1 cup fat-free vanilla frozen yogurt
- ¾ cup fat-free milk
- ¼ cup concentrate frozen orange juice

Directions:

1. Mix milk, frozen yogurt and orange juice in a blender, and blend until it gets smooth.
2. Add some ice into a tall glass and pour the smoothie into it.
3. Enjoy!

Nutrition: Calories: 160 kcal Total Fat: 2 g Total Carbohydrates: 34 g Fiber: 3 g Sugar: 24 g Protein: 5 g

Chapter 13.

21 Days Meal Plan

Day	Breakfast	Lunch	Dinner
1	Special Sausage	Chipotle Spiced Shrimp	Home Made Tomato Soup
2	Chili-Lime Grilled Pineapple	Scallop and Veg Skewers	Savory Pork Loin
3	Cod with Pearl Onions	Pork Chops with Tomato Curry	Marinated Salmon
4	Air Fried Branzino	Honey-Garlic Pork Chops	Savory Tomato Lentil Soup
5	Veggie Sushi	Hawaiian Salmon	Pork Tenderloin with Sweet Potatoes and Apple
6	Fruit and Nut Bar	Beef Stroganoff	French Country Chicken
7	Fruit Smoothies	Sesame Ginger Chicken Stir-Fry with Cauliflower Rice	Creamy Butternut Squash Soup
8	Snapper Fillets and Veggies	Curried Chicken wrap	Blackened Chicken with Berry Salad
9	Fruit Skewers with Vanilla Honey Yogurt Dip	Avocado Cucumber Soup	Marinated Salmon
10	Bell Pepper Mackerel	Savory Tomato Lentil Soup	Chipotle Spiced Shrimp
11	Spinach Salad with Walnuts and Strawberry	Home Made Tomato Soup	Pork Chops with Tomato Curry

12	Fruit Salad	French Country Chicken	Hawaiian Salmon
13	Lemon Sole and Swiss Chard	Blackened Chicken with Berry Salad	Curried Chicken wrap
14	Veggie Sushi	Pork Tenderloin with Sweet Potatoes and Apple	Avocado Cucumber Soup
15	Snapper Fillets and Veggies	Savory Pork Loin	Honey-Garlic Pork Chops
16	Spinach Salad with Walnuts and Strawberry	Creamy Butternut Squash Soup	Sesame Ginger Chicken Stir-Fry with Cauliflower Rice
17	Lemon Sole and Swiss Chard	Scallop and Veg Skewers	Beef Stroganoff
18	Chili-Lime Grilled Pineapple	Pork Chops with Tomato Curry	Savory Tomato Lentil Soup
19	Special Sausage	French Country Chicken	Avocado Cucumber Soup
20	Air Fried Branzino	Chipotle Spiced Shrimp	Curried Chicken wrap
21	Cod with Pearl Onions	Scallop and Veg Skewers	Savory Pork Loin

Chapter 14.

Frequently Asked Questions

By now you should have a well-rounded idea of what the DASH diet entails. You know the servings and types of food you should be eating, the foods to avoid, and how the DASH diet can benefit you. However, in case you have any longing questions, here are some answers and tips you can keep in mind as you start your journey to better health.

- **How difficult is it to stick to the DASH diet?**

The DASH diet isn't like other diets that you'll fall off of because of fatigue from restricting foods. Since the DASH diet allows for the consumption of a variety of foods, you won't get bored from sticking to a traditionally strict and restrictive diet. This is what makes the DASH diet a lifelong change for lifelong health rather than a quick fix to weight loss. With growing numbers of obesity in the world. The DASH diet is a way to curb these numbers without sacrificing your desired foods to eat. This is why the diet allows for 5 servings of sugar a week because we know those cravings will eventually come around, and moderate consumption is the only way to curb them.

- **Where can I buy food for my DASH diet? Do I need to purchase any supplements or pills to accompany the diet?**

Why the DASH diet is great is because it's accessible. You can buy all the ingredients for any recipe you want to make, under DASH guidelines, from the grocery store, farmers market, health store, or anywhere else you choose to buy your food from. There is no added supplements or gatekeeping in terms of ingredients you'd have to buy online. This diet involves only you, a new grocery list, and a trip to the market.

- **Do you need to exercise on the DASH diet?**

You do not need to exercise to see the health benefits of the DASH diet. However, exercise along with the diet can boost your health to the next level. Cardio along with strength training can allow you to burn more calories, lose weight, and reach your health goals sooner. Exercise doesn't have to be big, either. You can start as simply as walking for 30 minutes a day.

- **My blood pressure is good, should I follow the DASH diet?**

The DASH diet is formed to reduce blood pressure in those with high blood pressure. If you already have good blood pressure, this diet may not be right for you. Concepts of the DASH diet, like eating more vegetables and avoiding red meat can serve to help anyone. The diet ultimately focuses on healthy eating, which is a good lesson for people, high blood pressure or not. However, a more personalized diet that's targeted to your needs will fit those with good blood pressure better. Check with your doctor or physicians about other options for lifelong healthy eating diet plans that are suited for you.

- **When will I see the results?**

Many people following the DASH diet see results in lower blood pressure and weight in just 2 weeks. This depends on factors like your sex, starting weight, age, and more. However, the results do come fairly quickly with this diet and continue to benefit you throughout your time on the diet.

- **What can I drink on this diet?**

Water is always the go-to option for any diet, and this is no exception. Water hydrates while not adding extra calories or sugar to the diet. Watch that you're not consuming your calories in the form of drinks by drinking too much soda or alcohol while on the diet.

- **How long is the diet?**

This diet is designed to be a lifelong change for people that join it. The diet allows for occasional "cheat days" so you don't feel like you're completely missing out on the unhealthy foods you had before the diet. The DASH diet isn't a quick fix but rather a sustainable journey.

- **Why should you not eat processed foods on the DASH diet?**

Processed food has hidden additives like sodium and chemicals to keep the food fresh for longer. These are ingredients that are not allowed for the DASH diet as it may cause blood sugar to increase rather than decrease.

- **Do I need a DASH diet practice?**

It is recommended that you do 30 minutes of moderate activity on most days, and it is important to choose something that you like; in this way, you will more likely keep it up.

DASH diet is even more effective at decreasing blood pressure if combined with physical activity. Examples of moderate exercise include rustic walking (15 minutes per mile or 9 minutes per kilometer), running (10 minutes per mile or 6 minutes per km), cycling (6 minutes/mile or 4 minutes/km).

- **Can I drink alcohol while on a DASH diet?**

Too much alcohol can increase your blood pressure; in fact, it's associated with an increased risk of high blood pressure and heart disease to regularly drink more than 3 drinks a day. On the DASH diet, it is 2 or less for men, and 1 or fewer for women; you are required to drink alcohol sparingly.

- **Is the DASH diabetes diet safe?**

In contrast to often difficult to maintain faded diets, the DASH diet, which has long been promoted for its advantages in lowering high blood pressure, is also a top choice for diabetes care and is easy to begin. Let's look at what distinguishes it.

DASH stands for Dietary Approaches Stop Hypertension. Its main objective is to reduce blood pressure. Diabetes and high blood pressure tend to go hand in hand; over half of all adults with diabetes are diagnosed with hypertension. DASH diet may improve insulin resistance, high blood pressure and hyperlipidemia (an abnormally high-fat concentration in the blood), and obesity.

It works well on prediabetes and type 1 and types 2 diabetes because of the diet's weight, insulin sensitivity, and glycemic control. Research on the diabetes spectrum shows that the diet can reduce the future risk of type 2 diabetes by 20 percent.

- **Is DASH the same diet as Keto?**

The Whole 30, Dukan, and Keto diets are more restrictive on foods than DASH and the Mediterranean diets. This can make it harder for them to follow in the long run.

Chapter 15.
My Personal Recipes Notebook

Name of recipe: _____

_____

Serving: _____

Preparation time: _____

Cost: ☐ $ ☐ $$ ☐ $$$

Date: _____

Difficulties: ☐ low ☐ mid ☐ high

Cooking time: _____

Rating: _____

_____

List of Ingredients

_____   _____

_____   _____

_____   _____

_____   _____

_____   _____

Preparation

_____

_____

_____

_____

_____

Conservation

_____

_____

_____

_____

Name of recipe: _____   Date:_____

_____   Difficulties: ☐ low ☐ mid ☐ high

Serving: _____   Cooking time: _____

Preparation time: _____   Rating: _____

Cost: ☐$ ☐$$ ☐$$$ _____

List of Ingredients

_____   _____

_____   _____

_____   _____

_____   _____

_____   _____

Preparation

_____

_____

_____

_____

_____

Conservation

_____

_____

_____

_____

Name of recipe: _____

_____

Serving: _____

Preparation time: _____

Cost: ☐ $ ☐ $$ ☐ $$$

Date: _____

Difficulties: ☐ low ☐ mid ☐ high

Cooking time: _____

Rating: _____

_____

List of Ingredients

_____   _____

_____   _____

_____   _____

_____   _____

_____   _____

Preparation

_____

_____

_____

_____

_____

Conservation

_____

_____

_____

_____

Name of recipe: _____   Date:_____

_____   Difficulties: ☐ low ☐ mid ☐ high

Serving: _____   Cooking time: _____

Preparation time: _____   Rating: _____

Cost: ☐$ ☐$$ ☐$$$ _____

List of Ingredients

_____   _____

_____   _____

_____   _____

_____   _____

_____   _____

Preparation

_____

_____

_____

_____

_____

Conservation

_____

_____

_____

_____

Name of recipe: _____

_____

Serving: _____

Preparation time: _____

Cost: ☐ $ ☐ $$ ☐ $$$

Date: _____

Difficulties: ☐ low ☐ mid ☐ high

Cooking time: _____

Rating: _____

_____

List of Ingredients

_____   _____

_____   _____

_____   _____

_____   _____

_____   _____

Preparation

_____

_____

_____

_____

_____

Conservation

_____

_____

_____

_____

Name of recipe: _____   Date: _____

_____   Difficulties: ☐ low ☐ mid ☐ high

Serving: _____   Cooking time: _____

Preparation time: _____   Rating: _____

Cost: ☐$ ☐$$ ☐$$$ _____

List of Ingredients

_____   _____

_____   _____

_____   _____

_____   _____

_____   _____

Preparation

_____

_____

_____

_____

_____

Conservation

_____

_____

_____

_____

Name of recipe: _____

_____

Serving: _____

Preparation time: _____

Cost: ☐ $ ☐ $$ ☐ $$$

Date:_____

Difficulties: ☐ low ☐ mid ☐ high

Cooking time: _____

Rating: _____

_____

List of Ingredients

_____   _____

_____   _____

_____   _____

_____   _____

_____   _____

Preparation

_____

_____

_____

_____

_____

Conservation

_____

_____

_____

_____

Name of recipe: _____

_____

Serving: _____

Preparation time: _____

Cost: ☐ $ ☐ $$ ☐ $$$

Date: _____

Difficulties: ☐ low ☐ mid ☐ high

Cooking time: _____

Rating: _____

_____

List of Ingredients

_____   _____

_____   _____

_____   _____

_____   _____

_____   _____

Preparation

_____

_____

_____

_____

_____

Conservation

_____

_____

_____

_____

Name of recipe: _____   Date: _____

_____

Serving: _____   Difficulties: ☐ low ☐ mid ☐ high

Preparation time: _____   Cooking time: _____

Cost: ☐$ ☐$$ ☐$$$ Rating: _____

_____

List of Ingredients

_____   _____

_____   _____

_____   _____

_____   _____

_____

Preparation

_____

_____

_____

_____

_____

Conservation

_____

_____

_____

_____

Name of recipe: _____   Date: _____

_____   Difficulties: ☐ low ☐ mid ☐ high

Serving: _____   Cooking time: _____

Preparation time: _____   Rating: _____

Cost: ☐$ ☐$$ ☐$$$ _____

List of Ingredients

_____   _____

_____   _____

_____   _____

_____   _____

_____   _____

Preparation

_____

_____

_____

_____

_____

Conservation

_____

_____

_____

_____

Conclusion

Thank you for making it to the end. Initially, when the DASH diet was created, it was solely created to reduce and stop the spread of hypertension, but it was later discovered that people who adopted the DASH diet were able to lose weight to a considerable and moderate level. The reason for this was because of what the DASH diet entails that has made it effective for weight loss. As we end this book, here are some tips on how you can make your DASH diet work:

Remove processed and junk food from your refrigerator: With the DASH diet, it is required that processed and junk food is rid in the refrigerator because this food contains a high level of calories and unhealthy fats. Replace processed and junk foods with fresh fruits, vegetables, grains, and raw nuts. Throwing away junk food may seem too much to do; however, the best thing to do is refrain from buying them.

Prepare a grocery list: Before heading to the supermarket, ensure you have a list of the DASH diet food list to purchase. This is to help to refrain from what is not on the grocery list in respect to the DASH diet

Prepare your meal whenever possible: No matter how sweet and healthy a meal prepared in the restaurant is, you don't know the combination of the ingredients, whether it is a detriment to your weight loss or not. It is therefore important to ensure you prepare your meal all by yourself most times, and by so doing, you can monitor what goes into your body regarding the DASH diet

Stock your kitchen with DASH food: To avoid the temptation of eating foods that are detrimental to your weight loss, stock your kitchen with DASH food from time to time. By so doing, you get accustomed to the DASH diet

Avoid eating unhealthy snacks: Do away with snacks with unhealthy seasonings rather than go for snacks like popcorn cooked in olive oil and seasoned with garlic.

Consume less sodium: Food like bread, baked food, breakfast cereals, condiments, sauce, and canned products contain a high level of sodium, and these must be taken at the required level to avoid posing a danger to the bodyweight.

Checking of labels: Most people are victims of the act of not checking labels on food items purchased; thus, endangering their health. Check the labels of every food item in your kitchen and refrigerator, and dispose of anything that has a high intake of sodium, sugar, white flour, saturated or trans fats.

Portion control and serving sizes: This involves eating a variety of food in the right proportion and getting the required amount of nutrients needed. Eating to get overfed is what most people do all for the sake of eating to one's satisfaction, with this simple act, most people don't know that obesity can be gotten this, thus with the DASH diet, individuals know the amount of food to be taken with regards to the normal body functioning system and thereby, having a balanced body weight.

Avoid sedentary habit: This is a lifestyle that involves little or no physical activities. Examples of sedentary lifestyles are sitting with the computer all day long, reading all day long, or watching television most hours of the day. This kind of habit is not encouraged in the DASH diet, thereby not leading to unnecessary weight gain — more of a reason why the DASH diet encourages physical exercise.

I hope you have learned something!

Printed in Great Britain
by Amazon

18712549R00075